I LIVE IN A
CHICKENHOUSE

BOOKS BY MAX AMICHAI HEPPNER

THE LIFE IN HIDING SERIES

The Submergers
A father's story of escape and hiding from the Nazis

I Live in a Chickenhouse
A son's story of escape and hiding from the Nazis

A Guide for Teachers of the Holocaust
A son's story of escape and hiding from the Nazis

OTHER TITLES

A Vision of Love for Christians and Jews
The author's road to peace and forgiveness

Unexpected Encounters
Curing Jack Stickback & Other Stories

The Omer and the Kabbalah
Forty-Nine Blessings Leading to the Giving of the Torah

Max (Frans), about age 11

Max Amichai at age 84

I LIVE IN A CHICKENHOUSE

A son's story of escape and hiding from the Nazis

Third Edition

MAX AMICHAI HEPPNER

HEPPNER BOOKS

HILLSBORO BEACH, FL

Published by:
Heppner Books
HILLSBORO BEACH, FL
www.heppnerbooks.com

Copyright © 2007, 2020 Max Amichai Heppner

ISBN: 978-1-7348953-2-2

Map image on page xii by TUBS - Own work.
Based on File: Netherlands location map.svg by Lencer, CC BY-SA 3.0,
https://commons.wikimedia.org/w/index.php?curid=14339756

Cover and interior by The Book Couple, Boca Raton, FL

Printed in the United States of America

To the Janssen Family

The Janssens saved my life . . . and more! Thanks to them, I am a farmer with dirt under my nails . . . and a writer of books with clean fingers. I am a practicing Jew . . . and I know my catechism from studying with my Janssen sibs. They taught me to speak Brabant dialect . . . on top of my speaking Amsterdam Dutch.

The best gift I received from the Janssens, however, is unconditional love. I can go back to Brabant anytime, and they'll stop everything to welcome me home. Most of the older ones have passed on, but they transferred their love to the grandchildren and great-grandchildren. I know the Nazis hated me, but without intending to, they gave me the most loving family I could ever hope to be a part of.

No Child's Play:
Children in the Holocaust

"This [situation was] no child's play.
What matters is not what one plays with,
but rather how and what one thinks and feels while playing."

—JANUSZ KORCZAK, DIRECTOR OF THE JEWISH ORPHANAGE
OF WARSAW, POLAND, UNTIL 1942

---

*"No Child's Play" is the title of an exhibit
at Yad VaShem, Israel's Holocaust Museum.*

Max Amichai Heppner's childhood drawings are exhibited there.

Contents

Two Generations Recall Their Lives During the Holocaust

Even though I am a professional writer, I found it hard to write about my family's experiences in dodging Nazi persecution. My father's unfinished memoir and his notes, cartoons, and diary entries sat undigested in one pocket, and my own school essays, memories, notes, and drawings gurgled in another pocket. How could I handle all this material when it speaks in two different voices?

I found my own voice when I discovered drawings I had made as a child while I was in hiding. The drawings had the date on them of when they were made, and looking at the images brought me back to my thoughts and feeling from that time. That connection allowed me to write in the present tense, producing a book titled *I Live in a Chickenhouse*. The book is well suited for children, since I speak as a pre-teen and avoid much of the horror and fear in other Holocaust memoirs.

Early editions of *Chickenhouse* were published in the 1990s, and I decided recently to write an extensively revised edition. I was motivated by three reasons:

- I found new drawings and stories in my files;

- I intended to update and modernize the presentation; and

- I wanted to juxtapose my recollections as a child with those of my father as an adult.

Wanting this juxtaposition to stand out distinctly helped me write a companion book titled: *The Submergers, A father's story of escape and hiding from the Nazis.* That autobiographical story, told in the first person, reaches back to Father's life in Berlin, Germany, where he was born in 1900. He tells of his education in art history and his apprenticeship in business practices. However, he centers more intensively on his later years, from 1933 to 1945, when Nazi persecution caused him to increasingly feel a deep loss in status—from a respected Doctor of Philosophy to a mere shadow in hiding with a fake name.

Father (Albert) with son (Max) shortly after Liberation.

For comparison, my own *Chickenhouse* story begins in 1942; it extends into 1947, after the war ended and I moved with my mother to the United States. The *Chickenhouse* book and the *Submergers* book were produced and released together on www.amazon.com.

The original drawings used to illustrate the *Chickenhouse* story reside in the Jewish Museum of Maryland in Baltimore and good copies are exhibited at the Yad VaShem Holocaust Museum in Jerusalem, Israel.

Rediscovering My Childhood, a visual presentation of our survival story is on YouTube at www.youtube.com/watch?v=nM4CKksuK-ps&t=2s. Previews of other books are available on the author's website, www.heppnerbooks.com. Let us know how they affected you.

Max Amichai Heppner
Hillsboro Beach, FL
Third edition: October 2020

How I Came to Live in a Chickenhouse

For the first eight years of my life, I lived in Amsterdam, a big city in the north of Holland, or "The Netherlands," as we called it in school. In all that time, I never even visited on a farm, so you may wonder why and how I then came to live in a chickenhouse, way out in the countryside.

When I was eight years old, some "bad guys" burst into our apartment. They were Nazis. In loud, scary voices, they screamed orders at my mom. I was hiding in bed when they came. They stomped into my bedroom and tore through my closet but did't bother with me. When they left, they dragged off my mom. I still get the shivers when I remember how scared I was then.

That happened in August of 1942. Two years earlier, the Nazis had sent tanks from Germany into my country, Holland, and took everything over. They became increasingly nasty to the people of Holland, especially toward Jews. Mother, Father and I are Jewish, which is why the Nazis came after us.

They said we were no good and caused trouble. That wasn't true, of course. We lived our lives peacefully and got along well with our neighbors.

The Nazis didn't care whether we were good neighbors. They killed most of the Jews in Holland, including many children like me.

The total distance we traveled was less than 80 miles.

You could say I was lucky that they left me in my bed when they raided my home. My parents also were lucky. After locking Mother up for a couple of days, the Nazis let her go. Father hid in the attic during the raid and didn't get caught. When the three of us were back together, we decided to escape from Amsterdam along with the Graumanns.

The Graumanns were a Jewish family of three, just like us. The parents were Heinz and Elli, and their son was called Michael. I didn't know them well, but that changed when we went on the run together.

Father knew Heinz since they went to college together in Berlin. They went all the way for a doctor's degree, which was rare in their day. So they liked everybody to call them "doctor," which is common in Germany. In Holland, *doctor* means that you cure sick people, not that you studied art history, like Father did, or psychology, like Heinz did.

We moved from place to place for over a month because nobody let us hide with them for more than a few days. They were too scared to let us stay longer because the Nazis punished people severely if they were caught hiding Jews.

Even though we went to different places, we didn't travel far. You can see that on the map on the opposite page. At the end, we came to the Voorpeel at the edge of a swamp in a far corner of Holland. There we met Harry Janssen and family, who let us hide with them as long as we needed to.

With my pictures, I'll tell you stories about what I was feeling and thinking then. My thoughts were in Dutch because that's the language they speak in Holland. However, I'm telling my story in English, because that's what people speak in the United States, where I live now.

At first, it felt weird to live in the two very small rooms of a chicken-house on a faraway farm. Life there was about as different as you can get from my old life in an apartment in the big city of Amsterdam. After a while, though, I came to love living on a working farm out in the country. I hope my pictures and the stories that go with them give you a good idea what my life was like for the three years that I lived in a chickenhouse.

Sitting in the Sunny Corner

Today is March 20, 1943, and I am sitting on a bench behind the chickenhouse drawing the patio that we call our "Sunny Corner." It's barely warm enough to sit outside, even though I'm protected by the windscreen that Harry Janssen built for us. (Harry is the man who owns our farm.)

It feels especially good to be out in the fresh air after having been cooped up all winter. The winter seemed long, and it was dark and damp in our chickenhouse. We were lucky, though, that we had electric lights in the chickenhouse so at least we didn't have to sit in the dark with candles, like many people in the neighborhood.

Electricity is a new thing here, and it's especially rare to have a chickenhouse wired for power. We don't have switches or outlets to plug into inside the chickenhouse, however; we have only bare light bulbs. To turn the lights on or off, you have to turn the bulb in its socket.

The windscreen beside the chickenhouse.

That has its problems. One night I had to get up to go to the bathroom, which is in the stable next door. I reached up to turn on the bulb, but someone had taken it out instead of just loosening it. My fingers went into the empty socket, and, boy, did I ever get a jolt! I yelled so loud, everybody awoke and came running. I learned to check carefully whether there is a bulb in the socket, even when I'm very sleepy.

I'm glad to be outside today even though I'm not allowed to go beyond our patio with the wooden benches. It's okay for me to sit here because the windscreen around the patio keeps out more than the wind; it was built mainly to keep people from seeing us from the road when they pass our farm.

The patio is built against the side of the chickenhouse. The roof of the chickenhouse slopes, with the high end above the door. Inside, Father and his friend Heinz Graumann can stand up straight only at the high end of the chickenhouse, or else they bump their heads. They both are almost six feet tall.

Mother and Elli, Heinz's wife, don't bump their heads because they are shorter, and they can't go to the lowest part of the chickenhouse because furniture stands there. I am only nine years old now, and I'm short enough to stand up straight anywhere. I even could walk into the low end of the chickenhouse if it had no furniture in it.

When Father and Heinz bump their heads, which they do often, they yell in German. All of them sometimes talk German because they grew up in Germany. They moved out eight years ago, when the Nazis took everything over. Now, the Nazis have come to Holland also, and we all have to run away from them again.

Meeting the Janssen Family

Today it feels more like spring. It's April 24, 1943, and I'm sitting in the middle of our beet field doing my art project for today.

From here, I can see most of the buildings on our farm, except for the pig sty because it's built against the far side of the stable. So, I'm drawing a separate picture of where we keep the pigs.

To get from the Main House to the pig sty, you have to walk out the door of the kitchen parlor, cross between the Main House and the chickenhouse, and enter the sty from the other side.

The stable is part of the Main House. There is a brick wall between the stable and the kitchen parlor of the house to separate the people from the animals. The stable is home for our lone work horse, which they let me ride to the fields one time, and eight cows, which I'm learning to milk.

View of the Janssen farmstead (top).
The pig sty up against the Main House (bottom).

3

Between me and the other farm buildings sits the frame of the new barn that we are building. Life moves slowly on this farm, and the end wall of the barn is the only wall that's finished. It's been that way for months.

Right now, it's quiet on the farm. All five of us from the chicken-house—Father, Mother, Heinz, Elli, and I—are off doing something. We can get out of the chickenhouse as long as we go to places where nobody can see us from the road.

Through the barn window, which doesn't have any glass in it yet, I can see Heinz reading a book. Heinz and Elli live in the chickenhouse with my family, but they sleep in a bedroom in the Main House. They come here first thing in the morning, and they leave again at night when we all are ready to go to bed.

The Main House is the home of the Janssen family, who own this farm. Our farm is called *De Peelbloem* in Dutch, which means "Flower of *De Peel.*" Our neighborhood is called, *De Voorpeel* (or "Edge of *De Peel*"), and so the dirt road in front of our house is called *De Voorpeel Weg* (or "Voorpeel Road"). *De Peel* itself is the name of the marshy region, mostly swampland, near our farm.

Harry is the father of the Janssen family. His wife's name is Dina. They're both out working on the farm right now. Harry and Dina have nine children. The older ones are at school, a Catholic school in Deurne, the village nearest our farm. The younger ones are in the Main House.

Jan is the oldest of the Janssen children. He is twelve, three years older than I. He likes to act tough and always wants to fight me. I don't like him very much because he fights mean.

Annie, who is a year and a half older than I, is usually called *Zus.* That means "Sister" or "Sis." She helps take care of the younger children, who all look up to her.

Nel, also a girl, is nine, the same age as I. Fien, another girl, is eight. Mia is six. Then come two younger boys, Riek and Jo.

These two little boys are only four and three, but they're great about warning us if there ever are strangers in the neighborhood. When someone comes by unexpectedly, the people in the Janssen family tell one of the boys, "Little Jo (or Riek), why don't you go play out back." They know this means that they need to go to our chickenhouse and tell us to lay low and be extra quiet.

Martin was the youngest of the nine Janssen kids when we came. At the time, he was almost two years old. Then, just this month, a little baby was born, right in the farmhouse. I couldn't

Members of the Janssen family sitting in front of the chickenhouse, with Heinz (L) and my father (R) play-acting the role of "people in hiding" in a window. Sitting (L–R): Jan, Annie, Dina, Jo, Nel (partly hidden), niece Nellie, and Michelien on Dina's lap. Taken in 1943.

be there with the other children to watch her being born because the midwife wasn't supposed to know we're hiding here.

Annie says I didn't miss a whole lot. She says the birth of the baby wasn't all that different from when Loes, one of our cows, calved last winter. That time, Annie and I had watched together to see the calf come out.

When the midwife had left after helping to deliver the baby, Harry came to the chickenhouse with a huge smile on his face.

"It's a girl," he said proudly. Then he changed his voice to show he was adding something important.

"If you like," Harry said to Elli, "we'll make you and Heinz the new baby's godparents, and we'll call her Michelien. Then you can have another child to love and care for."

Later I asked Father what Harry meant by asking the Graumanns to be godparents for Michelien.

5

Father told me: "Catholic parents ask good friends to be godparents. If they accept, the baby gets named after them, even if they are of the opposite sex. Harry must have made up a special name for Michelien because I have never heard it before. And he must have made special arrangements with the priest in town, because godparents have to be present at the naming. Harry's priest must know who we are and keep quiet about it."

"So they'll take the baby to church for it?" I guessed.

"Yes," Father said. "The priest will pour holy water over the baby's head three times as he officially gives it a Latin name. They use Latin in church, just like we Jews use Hebrew for religious reasons, including names."

I imagined what the Catholic Church looked like.

"Really," I said amazed. "Names like Annie and Nel don't sound foreign."

"You're right," Father said. "Religious names aren't for every day. They sound foreign, like you said, and they are too long. Instead they use nicknames. Annie really was christened Johanna Maria Petronella; the *Annie* comes from Anna the end of Johanna. *Nel's* name is similar. Her Latin name is Petronella Maria Cornelia, and the Nel comes from the end of Petronella. All these names came from their godparents"

"Do godparents have to do anything for it?" I asked.

"Mainly, they have to make sure the baby gets a good Catholic upbringing," he replied.

I was going to ask; how could Elli and Heinz make sure that Michelien gets a good Catholic upbringing since they are both Jewish? But Father didn't look like he wanted to hear any more questions.

Getting Used to Brabant

I am sitting outside the Main House, and I can see Nel Janssen at the sink washing the dishes. We have an inside pump right at the sink, so we don't have to haul water to the kitchen from an outdoor well like most of the neighbors.

Nel Janssen washing dishes inside the kitchen parlor.

There are chickens all over the yard. The one in my picture is finishing off the crumbs Nel put out before she started washing the dishes. Riek gave the larger scraps to Foxie, the dog. We save everything that has a little food in it. After Nel finishes washing the dishes, she will give the rinse water to the pigs.

Just in front of the chicken is the cover of the *gier put,* or "manure pit." This deep hole in the ground holds manure from the stable. The window above it is the window of our only toilet since the toilet empties into the pit, too. Every few weeks, Harry hitches up the manure spreader to the tractor and spreads manure from the pit on one of the farm fields. The manure helps the crops grow.

Nel Janssen is almost exactly my age; she was born in July and I in October. We are good friends now, but when I first came, she stared at me.

"Who is this strange boy?" she asked her father, interrupting his conversation with my parents.

"It's your cousin from the city," Harry said, brushing her off.

"I don't know I had a cousin in the city, except for Ome Thy's children," Nel said boldly.

"Well, now you do," said Harry. "Why don't you children go in the yard and play."

We walked out the side door by the kitchen sink. Hardly anyone uses the front door that faces the street. That door is just for company.

Outside, Nel turned on me and poked a finger at my blue playsuit and said: "You look funny and you talk funny. In fact, everything about you is funny." And she looked me straight in the eye, daring me to say something.

To tell the truth, I thought *she* looked funny, playing outdoors in an apron. Aprons you wear inside the house. And I couldn't see where she came from, saying I talk funny.

Nel's way of talking didn't sound anything like I had ever heard before. I now know the language they talk here is called *Brabants*. The children learn proper Dutch in school, but they talk *Brabants* at home. It sounds so funny, I could hardly understand it at first.

I decided not to fight Nel about it. So, she thinks I look and talk funny and I think she looks and talks funny. So what. I said nothing and just looked back at her.

Her brother Jan gave me more trouble. He is a head bigger than me and poked his nose in my face.

"What's your name, city boy?" he asked.

"My n-name is M-Max," I said.

"Max!" he said, laughing. "Max is a dog's name! The new boy is a dog! Here doggie, doggie! Here Max, Max, Max."

I ran back to the Main House, sat down by myself on a milk stool in the stable, and thought things over. I could hear the grownups talking in the kitchen parlor, and I thought I could go to them. But they probably wouldn't take notice of me—they were so wrapped up in what they were discussing. I also heard the Janssen children still playing outside, and I decided I'd rather go back to them.

When I came outside, Jan took up right where we'd left off before. "You still have that funny name?" he asked, no friendlier than before.

"No," I said. I picked out a name on the spur of the moment. "My name is *Frans*."

"Frans," he repeated, and paused a minute. "Frans is a *good* name." Without another word, he picked up a ball and tossed it to me. We played catch and I wasn't so afraid of him anymore.

After a while, Mother called me inside. Before she could tell me what she wanted, I announced: "My name is *Frans*."

"What do you mean?" Mother asked.

"The children say that Max is a name for a dog. I don't want a dog's name. I want to be *Frans*."

"That's fine with me," Mother said. "Funny, that you children were talking about names. That's what we adults were talking about also. We'll all get new names, special names to use in hiding, and the Resistance will make us false identification cards. Our new cards won't have the big J on them." She was talking about the letter that shows we're Jewish.

"So remember," she said next, "now instead of Heppner, our family name is *Klein*. Instead of Graumann, Elli and Heinz will call themselves *Bergsma*. Our first names are fine the way they are—except for Heinz and you. Heinz will be *Jan Bergsma*. You said you want to be *Frans*, so you will now be *Frans Klein*. I'll tell Harry to have it put on your new identification card."

I wasn't sure I was happy about all these changes. Things were so much simpler when we lived back in Amsterdam.

Opa and Me

Today I'm looking at Father's drawing of Opa. He's my grandfather, and in Dutch we call grandpa *Opa*.

Father made this cartoon of me sitting on Opa's lap when I was a baby. I also want to draw a picture of Opa, but I can't. Tears keep getting into my eyes. I keep remembering how nice it was when Opa lived with us in our apartment in Amsterdam.

Opa's bedroom was in the front of our apartment, right next to my own bedroom. Mother and Father slept in the back part of the place. When I was a little boy, I took a sharp pencil and used it for several days to drill a hole through the wall between Opa's bedroom and mine. I wanted to be able to see him even at night because it made me feel safer.

In German, Opa asks the baby, "Would you like to go to Munich?" The baby replies: "No, no!"

My parents worked from home, and they used our dining room as their office. They had an art business. This means they sold old paintings, they gave lectures on art, and they wrote articles about it. For their customers, they kept an ever-changing exhibit of paintings on the walls of our sitting room.

My parents liked to have peace and quiet when they worked, so Opa would take me to the playground or on long rides on his bicycle, with me on the kiddy seat. When we came home, Father would grumble: *"Himmel, Donnerwetter, die Jugend kommt nach Hause."* ("Good heavens, the young crowd is home again.")

I liked going places with Opa, but that stopped when I was in Kindergarten. Opa couldn't live in our apartment anymore because he needed more care and had to an old age home. His new place is called *Klimop Huis,* which means "Ivy House" because of the ivy that covers the outside walls.

He had diabetes, for one thing, and Mother wasn't able to watch him enough. He'd sneak food that was bad for him. I saw him slip one cube of sugar after another into his tea when he took me along to the seemingly endless games of cards that he liked to play with his buddies.

At the Ivy House, there were nurses who could keep an eye on him all the time. The nurses also could help him clean up quickly when he couldn't get to the toilet in time. Then he didn't have to be so upset about it.

I think Opa liked the Ivy House well enough, but when I was in first grade, the Nazis made a rule that Jews and non-Jews couldn't live together in the same house any longer. They declared the Ivy House off-limits to Jews, even though it was near our Jewish neighborhood. Opa had to move to an all-Jewish home further into town. It is called *De Joodse Invalide,* or "Jewish Convalescent Home."

The new place was harder for us to get to. It became even harder when the Nazis took away our bicycles and made a rule that Jews couldn't ride on streetcars and buses any longer.

When we went into hiding, we had to leave Opa behind. He was too weak to run from place to place. He is probably is also too old to live in a chickenhouse, but I still wish he were here with us. I pray for him every day. I absolutely *want* him to still be in Amsterdam when we return there after the Nazis are gone and we can come out of hiding.

Father in His Business Clothes

Father made a cartoon to go with the letter he's writing to Ans and Frans. Ans and Frans aren't Jewish, and they are the only people back in Amsterdam who know where we are hiding. A secret messenger carries letters back and forth between us. His cartoon is making a joke out of trying to light our stove, but actually, lighting the stove in the morning is tough on him.

Father lighting our pot-bellied stove

It's windy out here in winter, and the wind often blows the smoke from the fire back down the chimney. All that smoke hits Father in the face when he tends the fire, and he comes gagging into the bedroom to get a breath of fresh air. Then he goes back and stirs and pokes the fire some more until he has it burning neatly.

Still, we are lucky to have a stove with fuel to burn in it. We burn peat, which is mined from the swamp land in our neighborhood. Peat is a mass of partially decayed plants that sits on top of the marsh. Peat can be hacked from the marsh, cut into little brick-like blocks, and stacked up to dry.

In olden days, people throughout Holland heated their houses with peat from *De Peel*. Now, most have switched to coal, but we still have peat on our farm. That's fortunate because there is no coal in the stores. Our peat blocks are stacked high between the new barn and our chickenhouse.

Father still wears his city clothes, even for messy work like lighting the stove. Even though his suit is showing wear, he puts on a shirt and a tie with it—everything neat as a pin. He says he doesn't feel dressed unless he wears the city clothes that he's used to. Me, I wear overalls and a shirt, just like the other children that live on our farm. It's much more practical.

When Father was still in the art business in Amsterdam, wearing business suits made sense. Even after the Nazis made him close his business, he was still "in business" in a way. They still allowed him to teach Jewish art at the Jewish Cultural Center.

One night, Father came home late from the Center, and that was the beginning of our big troubles back in the city. That night, Mother and I were holding supper for him, and we were just starting to really worry about him when he came in the door looking pale and scared.

"What happened?" Mother asked him.

"The Nazis were picking up Jewish men coming into our neighborhood," Father said. "They just pushed people into police vans. They didn't say why."

"How did you get away?" Mother asked.

"Joop, the butcher, warned me. He saw me walking by his shop and he gave me a 'Come here' sign through the window. I thought maybe he had saved a bit of meat for us.

"When I came into the store, he pulled me behind the counter. 'Get down,' he said. 'Stay back there. The Nazis are arresting your people.'

14

"Joop hid me in the butcher shop until the police vans had gone. That's why I am getting home so late."

He felt relieved that he escaped, but later that evening, the Nazi police came back again, sirens blaring. Through the window, we could see officers jump out of vans and cars and set up sentries at each corner of our block. Then squads went from door to door, to pick up more Jewish men.

Father jumped back from the window when he saw what was happening. He thought for a moment, and then told Mother he was going up to the attic and escape over the rooftops. He brushed by me without saying a word and ran out the living room door.

I went cold with fear. My parents had told me again and again *never* to climb out the attic window because it was so dangerous. Now Father would climb out and actually *run* across the rooftops!

The police soon barged into the downstairs door of our apartment building, and we could hear them tromping up the stairs. They yelled a loud *"Sieg Heil,"* a Nazi greeting, to the Kragts, our downstairs neighbors who were known as friends of the Nazis. Meanwhile, Mother quickly put me to bed, just throwing my clothes on a chair. I was going to ask why don't we fold them as usual, but Mother was in too big of a hurry to listen.

I hardly had pulled the blankets over me when they pounded on our apartment door. When they came inside, they shouted for Father to come. Mother said he wasn't home. They yelled that she was lying, and they searched all the rooms in the apartment, even my bedroom, but they left me alone. The whole time, I tried not to breathe and to keep myself motionless under my blankets.

I heard the police shout at Mother in German that it was her business to know where Father was and that they were going to arrest her for not telling. She asked, "Let me get my purse." They yelled, "No purse! Come! Now!" Then they pulled Mother out of the apartment and slammed the door.

My friend Rudy lived down the block. We had stayed friends even though he wasn't Jewish. Rudy's mother saw what was happening and came looking for me. She found me still hiding under my blankets.

"Max, come with me," she said, lifting the blankets from my head.

"No," I said, pulling the blankets back over my head.

"Please come," she said firmly and pulled the blankets off the bed.

"No," I said, pulling the pillow over my head. "I want my Mother and Father back. Leave me alone."

Finally, Rudy's mother jerked the pillow off me and made me put on my clothes again. She took me to her apartment, stood over me to make sure I undressed, and put me in the guest bed in Rudy's room. I hid my head under the pillow again, and I lay awake all night, worrying. I thought probably Father had fallen off the roof and Mother had been put in prison.

In fact, Father hadn't fallen off the roof. He hadn't even tried to climb out the window because he saw police with guns even on the rooftops. Instead, he hid in the attic closet where we kept our winter clothes. After the police left, in the middle of the night, he sneaked out of the apartment house and went to stay with our friends Ans and Frans Burbach.

The next day, Ans and Frans found out where the police had taken Mother and the other people who had been arrested. They had been placed in an empty theater because the prisons already were too full of Jewish people.

Now that it was clear where Mother could be found, Father and the Burbachs tried to get Mother a *Sperre*. A *Sperre* is what the Nazis call a document showing that a Jewish person is doing important work. With a *Sperre,* a Jew can get a delay from getting arrested for himself and his family. Since Father had been working as a teacher in Jewish adult education, Mother might be entitled to a *Sperre* and be released.

This plan worked. Our friend Ans went to Father's office and asked his boss to issue a *Sperre*. Ans took the risk of delivering it to the theater where the Nazis were keeping Mother. The Nazis screamed some more at Mother, but in the end, they let her go. In a few days, our family was all together again in our old apartment. But not for long.

Losing Beary-Bear

We left Amsterdam a few days after Mother was let go from prison, but at the time, I didn't know that we were running away from home. Father just said we were going into the country for a vacation. We packed in a hurry, and I forgot to pack my teddy bear whose name is *Beary-bear*. Outside on the street, I remembered. I turned back, but Father grabbed my arm.

"My Beary-bear!" I whined.

"Can't go back," Father whispered harshly. "The Kragts might hear us."

Father seemed mean about this. Today, I understand why. The Kragts, our downstairs neighbors, regularly used the Nazi salute, and we knew they were spying on us. If they found out that we were leaving town, they'd probably call the police. So that's why I couldn't go back for Beary-bear.

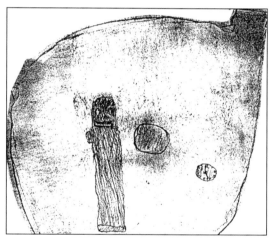

Friedje on our homemade nightstand

By now, the Nazis probably have found Beary-bear and shipped him off to Germany. To make myself a new toy, I carved a doll out of wood soon after we came to live in the chickenhouse. I call him *Friedje*. He sleeps on our nightstand, not like Beary-bear, who always slept in bed with me at our old apartment in Amsterdam.

As we left our old apartment with our suitcases, I still believed Father's story that we were going on vacation. It was August, vacation time, but soon I got the sense that this trip was not like any vacation we'd ever taken.

First, we walked to Wil Mautner's house. Wil is a friend of Father's who didn't live far from our apartment. When we got there, Father and Mother talked to Wil in very upset voices, and then Father did a strange thing. He took out his pocketknife, opened it, and ripped our Jew stars from our outer clothes. That seemed weird because ever since last spring, all of us Jewish people in Holland have to wear Jew stars on their clothes. It's a law.

A Jew star is a yellow piece of cloth with a Star of David design. Inside the star, the word *Jood* (Jew) is printed in funny letters that are supposed to look like Hebrew. Father wanted to burn all our stars, but Mother told him not to put hers in the fire. That way, she said, she could remember what it had been like to wear the darned things. She hid her old star in the lining of her purse.

I was going to ask why Father wanted to get rid of our Jew stars, but soon the answer was pretty obvious: We weren't going to wear them because we were going to ride a streetcar, which was forbidden. The Nazis had laws to keep Jewish people from riding on streetcars, buses and trains, and police checked everyone. They would arrest Jews who traveled illegally, and they could tell us apart even without stars because our ID cards had a big "J" stamped on them.

Later, I found out that Father and Heinz had planned out our trip ahead of time. We were all leaving Amsterdam about the same time, and they had arranged for scouts to look out for police so we wouldn't get arrested.

Obviously, the Graumanns also traveled without their Jew stars, and Heinz, like Mother, also wanted to remember how it felt to have to wear them. Instead of saving the stars, he saved a photo of them.

The Graumanns wearing their Jew stars: L–R Heinz, Elli, and Michael

The man who arranged a lookout for police was called Arie Heemert. I got to like him as I got to know him better—a really kind man. When we were going to get on a streetcar or train, his scout would get on ahead of us and give a secret signal if things looked safe. Arie also bought train tickets for our group ahead of time, so that we wouldn't even have to worry about being questioned at the ticket office.

My parents acted really nervous during our trip, but we were lucky—we didn't run into any police. Arie took us to Kockengen, a village only about 20 minutes from Amsterdam Central Station.

When we got there, Father finally told me what our trip was all about.

"It isn't safe for us to stay in our neighborhood in Amsterdam," he said. "There is no safe place there for Jews, and yet so many Jews live there. Kockengen is safer from the Nazis because very few Jews live in small towns like this. We are going to stay with Arie's family while Arie looks for ways for us to get even farther away from the big city."

We met the Graumanns briefly at the Kockengen station, but they immediately said goodbye. That surprised me.

"So where are the Graumanns going?" I asked.

19

"They're staying with a friend of Arie's at the other end of the village. Arie doesn't have room for everybody at his house," Father explained. "Michael will join them there."

The Heemert family had two boys near my age and lived in an old house near the center of the village. The village was quiet, and the weather was sunny. Soon our stay seemed more and more like a vacation after all. Everybody started to be less tense—until the police raid came.

It turned out that someone in Kockengen had told the Nazis that Jews were hiding there. Police surrounded the whole village and went looking door to door, questioning everybody.

Fortunately, we weren't home. I had gone camping with the Heemert boys on an island in the river outside the village, and my parents were out for a walk. They saw the police coming. Father hid in a dry ditch and Mother hid in a potato field. I was too far away to see or hear anything of the raid.

The police searched every house. Wherever they found Jews in hiding, they arrested them along with the people who had let them into their homes. When they didn't find any strangers at Arie Heemert's house, they looked disappointed, as if they had expected it to come out differently. Then they warned Arie's wife, Hilletje, that she shouldn't even think of hiding Jews at her house, or else her whole family would be in big trouble.

That night, Arie told us sadly that we would have to leave town, and that the Graumanns couldn't stay in town anymore either. He would hide our suitcases and we should walk out into the countryside with just our backpacks.

Arie walked us into the fields until we came across a cow shelter in a pasture. He left us there but said he would return the next day. There was hay in the shelter, and we spread it out to make beds. We lay down on the hay, but we stayed awake a long time, worrying about whether Arie really would come back.

I dozed off once, but I woke up when a big calf came to eat the oats left in the shelter.

Father chased the calf off with a shirt, play-acting like a bull fighter. I couldn't see how he could try to be funny when I was so scared. I was going to say something about that, and I wanted to know what Father thought would happen next. But it didn't seem likely I would get an answer. Lately, I don't seem to have a chance to ask about much of anything.

In the morning, a farm woman came to get the cows. She seemed surprised to see us in her cow shelter, but she turned around quickly and left without her cows. Moments later, she was back and handed us a basket of fruit. She didn't speak, and we didn't either. This time she took her cows and herded them to her farmstead.

Arie did come back. During the next three weeks, he hid us, together or singly, in all kinds of places. I spent time in a stuffy, empty attic room above a barbershop. Later, I stayed several days in the storeroom of a windmill with hundreds of sacks of grain. After that I hid out in a country inn that was closed for renovations. Next, all six of us wound up at the bathhouse of a Catholic summer camp. Finally, we went from there to the Janssen farm. That also was supposed to be just a temporary hideout. But fortunately, Harry Janssen decided to let us stay.

Losing Michael

This morning, June 26, 1943, I have the chance to be alone in the bedroom of the chickenhouse and sketch in peace. The one interesting thing to draw here is Elli's desk that Heinz (whom we really should be calling Jan now) recently made for her. He took a piece of board, smoothed the edges, and attached wires to hang it against the wall.

Elli keeps her things on the desk—a notebook, a hot water bottle, pocketbook, and a photo of Michael. I see that she took along Michael's picture, probably to cry about it somewhere where she can be alone.

Elli has been in all kinds of strange moods lately, and her attitude towards me especially has its ups and downs. Sometimes she suddenly calls, "Come here, *Liebchen*," which means "Dear" in German; then she strokes my head and takes out her factory-made weaving needles and helps me weave baskets. She won't

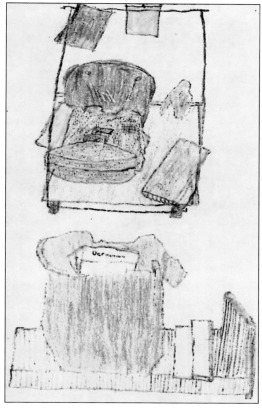

Elli's personal desk and possessions.

let me use her fancy needles, but I'm okay with using the needle I made from a bent wire.

Other times, Elli acts really mean towards me. She pushes me away and then says to Father, in a bitter voice, "How come you deserve to have that brat of yours when my wonderful son is rotting away in a grave?"

It's not surprising she's so moody, because what happened to her son, Michael, is really awful! He got killed practically in front of our eyes.

It wasn't even the Nazis who killed him. It was an acquaintance of Arie, the man who helped us escape from Amsterdam.

I met Michael about a year ago when our mothers became close friends by going shopping together. When we still lived in Amsterdam, the Nazis made it hard for Jews to buy food and clothing. Jews were not allowed into stores before 4 p.m., the end of the day when most of the goods had already been sold. For every bit that was still available, we had to wait in line. The lines were long, and Mother and Elli shared the wait.

Photo of Michael that Elli treasured.

When I met Michael, he was 15 and I was only 7. He enjoyed showing me tricks that big boys can get away with. For example, one hot summer day, he showed me how he swipes ice chips from the iceman, who delivers ice for icebox that the Graumanns use to keep food fresh. The ice in the cooling compartment slowly melts of course, and the iceman has to bring fresh ice regularly.

When Michael wants ice chips, he waits while the iceman goes to the back of his truck to chop his big blocks of ice into smaller pieces. This leaves a lot of chips. So, while the iceman makes his delivery to their apartment, Michael grabs what chips he can, and makes a run for it.

The day Michael showed me the trick, I couldn't reach into the ice truck because I was too small. Michael boosted me up, and then I could reach even further into the truck than he. I scooped up all the chips I could hold, and with chips melting in our fingers, we ran behind the apartment house. There we leaned against the bike rack, enjoying the cool crunch of the ice chips.

But I didn't hang out much with Michael when we lived in Amsterdam. I got to know him a lot better after we all left Kockengen and wandered together from shelter to shelter. Sometimes Arie Heemert, who guided us, put the grownups in one place and us boys in another. After three weeks of this, Arie turned us over to Henk Brandhorst and Jose Peerebooms. They were part of a group of smugglers.

Jose, I hadn't met before, but I knew Henk because he had sheltered the Graumanns while Mother, Father, and I had been staying with the Heemerts. Arie said they were smuggling gasoline from France, and on their return trip there, they would smuggle us south in the gasoline truck. The part of France where they went was called *Free France* because the Nazis hadn't completely taken it over. You could still make arrangements there to escape to America.

It would take a few days to get the truck ready, so Jose had all six of us stay in the bathhouse of a swimming pool. The pool was part of a summer camp owned by a group of Catholic monks. At the time, no campers actually stayed on the place. Occasionally, some monks came to swim, but even though they had arranged for us to be there, they never said a single word to us. They just acted as if we weren't there.

In many ways, the summer camp was a pleasant place to live in because we could go swimming as much as we wanted and we could do laundry.

We only had one set of clothes with us. When they got dirty, Mother would tell me to just get dressed in my underwear. She'd wash my shirt and pants, and when they had dried in the sun, I'd wear them on my bare body while Mother washed my underwear!

We cooked some at an open fireplace, but most of our food was carried in by a runner from a local restaurant. He was just a young boy. He'd slip in quietly from the forest, drop off our covered dishes without a word, and slink away before we hardly realized he had come and gone.

But pleasant as it was, we knew we couldn't stay at the summer camp for very long. There was no heater in the bathhouse, and the nights were getting cold. At the same time, the monks were getting nervous about our staying at their camp so long. They sent us a note that people in the neighborhood were starting to wonder out loud about the runner carrying all those restaurant meals into the woods.

All the time we were at the camp, the smugglers kept stalling about when they'd be bringing their truck to take us South. Every time, they had another excuse. When we'd get really impatient with them, Jose would squelch us. Jose always was full of stories in which he was the hero who could get anything done, and he acted like getting us into Free France by truck was the easiest thing in the world. "You can trust me," he'd say to Father.

But Father didn't trust Jose. Several times, I heard the two of them argue over money. Jose wanted to be paid in advance, but Father said, no. He gave Jose part of the money, and Father said he'd pay the rest only after the trip was over.

Eventually, Father and Heinz told Jose flat out that it just wouldn't work for us to stay at the camp any longer. Jose seemed to understand they were serious, and he promised to find us another place to hide while he finished arranging for the truck.

We now know that instead of carrying out these arrangements, Jose and Henk made plans to kill us. I think they thought it would be quicker and easier to steal our money than to earn it by leading us to safety in France.

At the time, however, the smugglers acted as if everything had been properly arranged. They said that they had found a new hiding place and would move us one or two at a time, as usual, to lessen the chance of our being heard or seen by outsiders.

In the morning of the agreed-on day, they came for Michael, who was to go out first. That's the last I ever saw of him. And that's the last Elli saw of him, which is why she hangs on to his photo.

It was only several weeks later that Arie told us how Michael died. The day before Jose and Henk planned to move us, they had dug graves for all six of us at the back of the camp. When they took Michael past that place, they killed him by hitting him over the head with a hammer.

I don't know why they decided *not* to kill the rest of us. Apparently, Harry Janssen had something to do with it because the smugglers brought the rest of us to a crossroads in the countryside, where Harry took us over.

The same day that we found out what had happened to Michael, the adults went back to the camp to see Michael's grave, but they wouldn't take me. They said it would be too scary. They were wrong. I was so scared then that seeing the real truth would have been a relief.

Bickering in the Chickenhouse

Today, Mother is really upset from the strain of the bickering that has started. Both Heinz and Mother want to stay out of the fight, I think, but they don't say anything about it. In fact, they say very little of anything, and now it's quiet around here like a cavern.

The trouble started when Elli started to blame Father because Michael is dead. When Elli first started picking on Father, she took us all by surprise. She was looking at her picture of Michael, studied it intently, then got Father's attention.

Mother, drawn by Heinz Graumann.

"Albert," she said. "Tell me. Wasn't Michael a wonderful boy?"

"Yes, Elli," he said. "He was a fine boy."

"So, don't be so short," she said. "Tell me more. Tell me how wonderful he was."

Father paused, not really knowing what to say. Then he said, "Elli, I know how much you miss him. I know how much he meant to you. Nobody can put that into words better than you."

Elli hardly seemed to listen. "You try," she said. "You try. I've got to hear you say it. Come on. Tell me why you agree that he was an incredibly great person."

Father squirmed, and I know why. He had been pretty angry with Michael before he died.

There had been a lot to do at the Catholic priests' camp where we had all stayed together for several weeks. Michael was strong, but lazy. He sneaked away, for example, when it was time to chop wood. When Father called him out on it, he just opened a smart mouth.

29

After that, Father left him alone, but I'm sure he wasn't happy about it.

Now Father had to tell Elli that this boy was the greatest hero that ever came down the pike. He couldn't honestly do this, I think.

He cleared his throat and said, "Elli, he was a fine boy. You loved him a lot. Let's just leave it at that."

At that, Elli turned furious. "You just don't want to say it," she yelled sharply. "You want to rob me of every tiny little bit of comfort." By then, she was screaming: "You have a hard heart, Albert. I can see it right through your chest. Your heart is hard as stone, as uncaring as granite."

Father, drawn by Heinz Graumann.

She flashed her dark eyes at Father, whirled past him, and went out the door. I didn't see her the rest of the day. Obviously, she went to bed and stayed there.

The next morning, she was cold, icy cold. No matter what she said to Father, she put a mean word into it. Like, when she asked Father to pass her the salt for breakfast, she'd add: "If it isn't too much trouble for a man like you who doesn't even have a kind word for a woman who lost her son."

Father hated that and insulted her right back. They stayed angry until today. Mother and Heinz seem to appreciate when it's quiet. I think they're afraid that no matter what they say, either Elli or Father will start up with that wacky fight of theirs again.

I suppose that's also why Father started to go on long walks. For a while, he went out at 3 o'clock in the morning. I wanted to go along because when we lived in Amsterdam, Father didn't have much time to spend with me. He worked long hours during the day, and at night, he wrote articles. When we started walking together in the middle of the night, we could just walk and talk. We thought 3 a.m. would be safe enough, but the baker saw us and said don't do it, it's too dangerous. We stay on the farm, but we still talk.

School Lessons on a Wintry Day

Today Father is in the bedroom talking to Mother. She is trying to keep warm by snuggling between the red blanket and the warm straw mattress under her. There is no heater in the bedroom, so the bed is her best way way to keep warm.

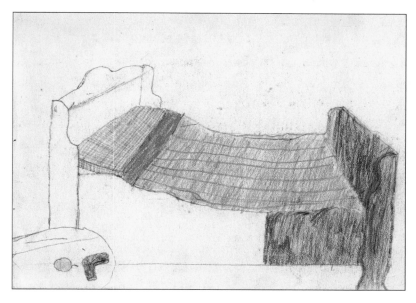

Mother and Father's bed

I am waiting for my school lessons to start. I'm sitting with my back to the stove, so I can keep nice and warm, drawing pictures and looking at my books. I have only four books, besides my textbooks for home schooling. I read the same books again and again, and I also draw the pictures in them.

I love one with drawings and poems about animals, and I made pictures of some of the strange-looking ones. The one about the zebu says (in Dutch):

From English India comes the Zebu.
It looks a bit just like our cow.
It gives good milk and is quite strong,
And helps the farmer with his work.

I haven't gone to a regular school since I attended the Jeker School in Amsterdam. When I was in kindergarten, all of us were together—Jewish or not Jewish, it didn't matter. But the Nazis wanted it different. About half of us in the Jeker School were Jews, so they built a wall from the attic clear down to the first floor. There was no door to connect the two sections. My first-grade class in the Jewish section had a separate entrance and a separate playground.

Nel would gift me saints trading cards.

The Janssen children go to Catholic school and, of course, there are no Jewish children there. They bring me gifts home from school to make me feel better about having to stay home. Their greatest gift was sharing oranges the time when the Red Cross suddenly delivered a load of them for the kids. Instead of gobbling up their oranges, the kids saved them and brought them home to share. I got several sections and just loved the treat. I saved a piece of rind under my pillow for days, and took a little nibble every morning to remember the taste.

Now in the chickenhouse, we have home school every day. We do all the regular school subjects first, such as Dutch composition and grammar, which we both enjoy, and math, which we both hate. But Father says, "At least learn your multiplication tables. It will help you do the arithmetic quickly when you have to figure prices, like I have to for my art business."

My foreign language for school is English. Of course I also am learning German, but that's informal—in fact, everyone pretends no German is being spoken here at all. But that's crazy! I've heard German spoken ever since I was a baby. Opa spoke it all the time with his friends.

Now my parents and Elli and Heinz speak German among themselves when they don't want me to know what they're talking about. They really don't seem to realize I understand almost everything they say. The more they discuss secrets in German, the harder I work to understand it!

My favorite subject is art, and Father promised to give me regular drawing lessons if I do well on my other school subjects. For himself, Father likes to draw cartoons, and I asked him to help me do one of those.

"Glad you're interested," Father said, "I've had fun with cartoons ever since I was in my twenties."

He drew me a cartoon of him bow-ing to be helpful and a funnier one of himself doing a drawing. He splashed an ink blot on it on purpose and said, "You can even learn something from a blot like this—you can learn to do it better the next time." We both laughed!

"For now," he said then, "let's stick to basics and draw things the way they look in real life. How about we start with *klompen* for today's lesson? They're good practice for drawing three-dimensional, rounded objects."

Klompen are wooden shoes that farmers and fishermen wear. I saw *klompen* now and then when I still lived in Amsterdam. For example, a man who worked in

The Dutch says: "Perhaps you'll learn something from drawings like these."

the fish store used to wear them. Before I moved in with the Janssens, I never would have thought that one day I would be wearing *klompen* myself. But I got used to them fast.

The main problem with wooden shoes is that it's just about impossible to run in them. We kick them off for running games, especially in warm weather. One day last winter, however, Jan Janssen boasted that he could run without *klompen* through the snow all the way to the Aarts house next door and back. He did it, too, that big show-off! I myself wouldn't try it. I keep my wooden shoes on when it's cold outside.

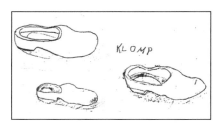

Drawings: *klompen* (top), men walking (center), the birthday box (bottom)

Our lesson went on with Father showing how to make it seem that people are in motion even though they're in a still picture. Father drew different body parts and showed how they change position when people are moving. Together, we drew pictures of a man who is walking. Then, Father drew a complete picture with people in motion. For his subject, he chose Riek and Little Jo carrying our *Birthday Box.*

The Birthday Box is a part of a routine we invented ourselves. We put all the presents into a big old soap box, and Little Jo and Riek have the honor of carrying it into the party room on a couple of poles.

Father put *klompen* and people in motion into another lesson; he started by making a drawing of a woman in *klompen* hanging the laundry.

The woman in the picture (next page) is Hanneke, Harry's sister-in-law. She, her husband, Piet Janssen, and their six children moved onto our farm a couple of months ago.

I enjoy working with Father, but still, sometimes he gets mad at me. One day, I was out playing in the fields with the Janssen kids when it was time for lessons. Father called me, I couldn't hear him, he couldn't see me, and he panicked.

Hanneke Janssen hanging the laundry.

When we got back to the farmyard, he was furious. He yelled at me and just wouldn't stop. He said the same things over and over: "If it's time for your lessons, you are to be there!" And then, "I want you to keep in sight of the farmyard, even if you go out into the fields." And also: "Don't you know that running away can be dangerous?"

He was so angry, that he whacked me hard on the behind. That's unusual; he had never struck me before. And he kept on grumbling, even when we had already started with our lesson.

I always put my name and the date on my schoolwork, just like I did in regular school. You can see that on my drawings. Father asks me to do this, even though here I am the only student. So as usual, I started writing the date. It was 4- 4-'44, the fourth of April in 1944.

I said to Father, "Isn't that neat! All 4's in the date today."

That brightened him up. "Can you figure out how often that happens?" he said. "All numbers in the date, the same! It's really a rare thing." And all of a sudden, he was his old, friendly self again.

35

Why I Call Myself Frans

Father likes to use cartoons he made in the past to tell me about old times. The one I'm looking at today is of him at a masked ball, a kind of dance where everybody dressed up in a costume, often including a mask. Part of the fun is guessing who each person at the dance is pretending to be.

Father and Ans at the Bellevue Hotel ball (left).

Below is the letter I wrote Ans and Frans with thanks for the presents they sent me.

Dear Aunt Ans and Uncle Frans,
Thanks for the belated St. Nicholas Day presents. The poem that Uncle Frans wrote wasn't too great. I liked the presents a thousand times better.

The book you sent about Till Eulenspiel was the best, and it made me laugh so loud that Father scolded me for making too much noise. But Father was happy to work with me on the geography book you sent. We have just reviewed all the Dutch provinces.

For Mother's St. Nick's present, I made a pin cushion. I took a little match box, decorated the outside, and lined the little drawer inside by wrapping a piece of cloth with some sheep wool that I found hung on a barbed wire fence.
Love,
Frans

This particular dance is important to Father because that's where he met his friend Ans. Back in February of 1925 (the date on the cartoon), Father was studying in Amsterdam. He was living by himself and needed to make some new friends.

Ans was also feeling lonely, and it so happened that each of them decided to go to a dance at the Bellevue Hotel. Father was dressed as a Turkish prince and Ans pretended to be a Turkish princess. They matched. Father thought this was interesting. He told her so, and that's how they started talking and became friends. After Father married Mother and Ans married Frans, all four of them became friends.

It's nice for me to have Ans and Frans as friends, as well. I decided to call them my godparents after I found out that all the local kids have them. Since I picked the name *Frans* for myself, it seemed logical that Frans Burbach would be the godfather after whom I was named. By the same logic, Ans would be my godmother. They have no children of their own, and they call me *Zeun,* which is Brabants for "Son." I call them Aunt and Uncle: *Tante Ans* and *Oom Frans.* I am so happy that they sent us nice gifts for St. Nick's Day, even though they arrived three weeks late.

Father reviewing his news reports in bed.

One of my gifts was an old atlas. Now Father uses maps in that geography book to compare with battle maps that we cut out of the newspaper. We follow exactly how far the Allies are advancing in the war against the Nazis. We have done so, battle by battle, ever since they won their first big fight against the Nazis, at El Alamein in Libya. You can see Libya at the very bottom of the map of Europe from my old atlas; there they use the former name for the country, *Tripolis*.

Map of Europe and the Mediterranean.

To keep me interested, Father promised me a quarter for every place that the Allies take from the Nazis and I could find in my atlas. Kiev, a town in Russia, is on that same map of Europe, and it was retaken by the Germans and recaptured by the Russians twice more, so I claimed seventy-five cents. Father paid off once, but said, never again; one quarter per town and that's that. And he explained that all that fighting was terrible for the people that lived there. "So," he said, "let's not make too much of a game of it."

Father also used my maps to explain the war news to other people on the farm. Then he started writing a news summary on his typewriter, and Harry had the Resistance make copies for their supporters. That lasted until one copy fell into the wrong hands, and the police tried to trace where the news reports came from. They never traced the reports to Father, but he still decided he had better stop distributing his news reports. We still follow them on the maps, however.

Drawing Things
in the Chickenhouse

Today, December 30, 1943, I'm by myself in the chickenhouse living room, drawing the things I find around me. The peat barrel is on my right and the stove is behind me, out of sight. My pencil and crayons are in front of me, and my sketchbook is further forward on the table.

View from the living room table.

You can see on the drawing that one pane in our living room window is broken. Father mended it with cardboard. Glass is hard to get these days, even if you have the money to pay for it. Harry still hasn't put panes in the windows of the new barn.

They haven't even been able to replace the pane that Nel and I broke in the Main House when we had a fight with coal eggs. Coal eggs are made from compressed coal dust formed into egg-shaped balls and are good for making a peat fire hotter.

Nel started the fight. When I threw the coal egg back at her, she ducked and the coal egg hit the window. Dina, her mother, heard the glass splintering, and she yelled at both of us.

"He broke the glass," Nel said, pointing at me.

"She started," I said, pointing back at Nel.

"I don't want to hear any more of this," Dina said. "I don't care who did what. If two people fight, they're both at fault. You'll both pay for the glass when we can get some." She took the money in advance from our piggy banks.

I wonder whether what Dina said about fights applies to the war that the Americans and British and the other Allies are fighting with the Nazis. Everyone I know blames the Nazis for everything bad that's happening in Europe. If Dina is right, do the Allies also deserve some of the blame?

Just as we don't have glass for windows, we don't have proper materials to build a storm door. Trying to keep drafts out of the chickenhouse, Father and Heinz built a cardboard screen for the entrance. It was a nice idea, but it doesn't do much good. However, we kept the screen in place even last summer because we thought it might help keep out the flies. Actually, the screen doesn't do much against flies, either. Neither does anything else we try against them, including the sticky paper we hang up.

I tried to eat a slice of bread with honey when the weather first turned warm, and the honey turned black with flies before I could take a second bite. Since then, I've been folding bread with honey into a sandwich. That way, I only have to chase the flies from the edges where the honey runs out.

After I was done drawing things in the living room, I moved to the bedroom to find something new. I considered drawing my bed, but I didn't feel like it. It's really just an old baby crib. Harry brought it to the chickenhouse the day we moved in.

"That's for you, Max," he said. I still was called Max then. "You like it?" he asked.

I didn't know he was teasing me, so I said, "I can't fit into that. It's for a baby."

"Aw, you can just curl up real tight and you'll sleep like a prince," he said.

I still didn't realize he was putting me on, and I must have shown that I was really worried.

Harry laughed. "Naw," he said, "I will make a real bed out of this for you."

He took off most of the sides and extended the bottom. It still looks like an old baby crib but I can sleep stretched out.

What was left to draw was stuff we store in the far corner. When we came here, we only brought the few things that we had in our backpacks. Now we have lots more stuff.

After the Janssens decided to let us stay with them, Arie brought us suitcases full of things that we had left with him. Then, Ans and Frans sent us other things, such as Father's *Hermes Baby,* a portable typewriter. Mother got back her old sewing kit. I got my art supplies.

The storage corner.

43

In my drawing, you can see Father's pajamas hanging from a hook and my toy train on the floor between a pair of old wooden shoes. Obviously, Father and Heinz don't do well at carpentry, as you can see by the crooked legs on the little bench where my boots and my knapsack stand. The shelf they built along the wall is uneven, but it works. Crooked or not, it holds our stuff off the damp floor.

Making Peace with Heinz

einz is a good artist. He recently painted our neighbor, Hannes Manders, sitting in his kitchen parlor by the stove. Father said, "It looks a lot like a painting by Vincent van Gogh. It's my favorite."

Hannes Manders, warming himself by the stove by Heinz Graumann.

Today, I looked on as he painted the way the Driek Aarts farm next door looks from here. Naturally, he couldn't paint it from up close, where he could be seen by people passing by. I like seeing him paint, and I am happy he didn't shoo me away.

Heinz stopped, and out of a clear blue sky, he asked, "Do you like that Till Eulenspiel book that they sent from Amsterdam?"

"Sure," I said. "I loved the story about that fool. I finished it yesterday."

View of the Aarts farm by Heinz Graumann.

"But you got the book only the day before. You couldn't possibly have taken it all in," Heinz said.

"I read fast," I answered, "but I remember everything. Test me if you like."

Heinz liked the challenge and so did I; he didn't catch me on anything I missed. I liked his quiz even better because he stopped being so cold towards me.

We talked some more. He turned back to his work, and then he turned to me and asked: "Do you like this scene?"

"I like farm scenes," I said. "You do them well."

"You do good farm scenes yourself." Heinz said, "but these days, I'm interested in also doing portraits. Would you like me to do one of you?"

It's a relief that Heinz is acting friendly again because, for a while, he would bawl me out for no reason at all.

My parents had an argument with Heinz about this one evening. They were in the living room, and they were trying to keep their voices down because I was supposed to be sleeping in the bedroom next door. Because I had to strain to hear what they were saying, I sneaked out of bed and listened with my ear against the door.

"Heinz," Father said in a loud whisper, "I want you to leave Frans alone. He is my boy. If he misbehaves, I'll take care of it. If *you* think he needs correcting, you tell *me!*"

"Oh," Heinz came back sarcastically. "You think you're doing such a great job raising that boy! Well, let me show you something."

Suddenly, Heinz jerked open the bedroom door that I was leaning against, and I half fell into the living room.

"So much for your wonderful child-rearing methods'" Heinz said to Father. "How about, you start your next project by teaching him not to snoop."

He turned on his heels, walked stiffly to the outside door, and slammed it behind him.

Father didn't punish me. He just gently led me back to bed, covered me up, and said: "Go to sleep, my boy. We'll talk about this in the morning."

In the morning, Father didn't say anything more about it, but Heinz just started giving me the cold shoulder. Now he even gave me his "View of the Aarts Farm." I feel lucky to have it, and not just because it made me feel better about him. I also am proud because this painting has made Heinz famous.

Portrait of Frans.

47

Before he gave the painting to me, he showed it to Driek Aarts. He was pleased and asked Heinz to paint his farm again, this time with a close-up view of the house. Driek offered to let him paint in a shed where people couldn't see him from the street.

When Heinz was done, Driek showed the painting to his friends. Soon many more people asked for a painting of their own farmhouse.

It actually was Harry's brother Thy who started a fad about it. He said a farmhouse painting would be a perfect gift for his niece, Nel, who just got married. If she could hang a picture of her parents' house in her new home, she'd feel less homesick.

That became Heinz' selling point. Other daughters about to be married (and even daughters who were already married) wanted pictures of their old homesteads. So Heinz has a regular business now, selling paintings for wedding presents. He paints most homesteads from photographs that people bring him.

"Stick to your lessons," Heinz told me. "You never know how what you learn can come in handy."

About Chickens and Eggs

Today, December 31, 1943, I'm sitting by the window looking outside for something to draw. They finished harvesting our beets just a few days ago, and a cart full of beets is still standing in the yard. There's a chicken beside the cart, and I'm watching to see if the chicken will take a peck at a beet that dropped on the ground. The chicken is moving on, so it probably doesn't like beets.

Chicken by the beet cart.

Cattle like beets, though. I'm surprised that they can chew them because cows have teeth only in their lower jaw. I asked Harry about it. He showed me that cows have a hard ridge on their gums for uppers. They can mash and crunch the hard beets against this ridge in their mouth by moving their lower jaws from side to side.

The only chickens we still have left are a few hens that roam free in the barnyard, like the one that was pecking around the beet cart. They nest mostly in the shed, although they make temporary nests wherever they can scoop one out. We kids try to find all the nests and bring back the eggs. We have fun with our egg hunts.

When I think about eggs, I am reminded about how much my Opa used to love eggs. He liked them soft-boiled, served in a porcelain egg cup. He had a special egg spoon, which is tiny, like a baby spoon, so you can easily take out the white that sticks to the shell.

"Ein Ei lässt sich nimmer erschöpfend leeren" (An egg can never be completely scooped out), he used to say in German, while spooning out the last bit.

A new group of baby chicks has just hatched. I saw a few peck their way out of their shells. It is fun to hold a newly hatched chick in the palm of your hand—carefully, so you don't crush it. It feels like a soft little ball of fluff.

Now the new chicks are pecking around the yard, just like the old hens. When they start laying next winter, Harry will kill the old hens—just as he did last year. He wrings their necks or chops off their heads. We keep one or two for chicken soup, but we sell the rest on the *black market.*

The black market is where you sell things secretly. If the Nazis know you have food to sell, they steal it or they just take it and only pay very little money. So, Harry says, the best thing to do with extra food is to sell it "black."

When Harry chops the head off his chickens, they often flap their wings afterwards. I once saw a headless chicken flap its wings so hard that it flew right over our haystack.

That got me to wondering what it is like to be killed. When Nazis kill people, do they also chop off their heads? Harry says he chops the heads so fast, the chickens don't even feel it. Would that be true for people as well? Would people with their heads chopped off flap their arms like chickens do with their wings?

Feeding All Twenty-Four of Us

It's still the middle of winter. As usual, Father relit the potbellied stove in the living room of the chickenhouse this morning. Now he's toasting bread for breakfast on the baking sheet he and Heinz made for the top of the stove lid. Toasting the bread helps make it taste better. If you don't toast it, the bread we get nowadays tastes like glue.

Our potbellied stove with some toast in the making.

One day last summer, Fien, Riek, Nel, and I took some of these squishy loaves into the yard, kneaded them into balls, and had an out-of-season snowball fight. It was great fun, but the adults got angry. They yelled at us, saying that we were wasting several days' worth of breakfast.

51

Except for us making our own toast, Dina, does all the cooking on the cook stove in the kitchen parlor. Still, we help prepare food for cooking, which makes it easier for Dina. Since Piet Janssen's family came to live in the other chickenhouse, we are now feeding 24 people.

We eat a lot of potatoes. To feed all 24 folks on the farm, that means we have to peel four full buckets of potatoes, every day. We also unstring green beans, take peas out of the pod, scrape carrots, and sew tobacco leaves on strings. Of course, we don't *eat* tobacco. Harry dries strings of it in the new barn to cure it, and then he sells it on the black market, the same way he sells chickens.

Harry also sells hogs on the black market. If perhaps you think it's gruesome to see Harry kill chickens, don't ask how he does it to hogs!

He ties one leg of a live hog to a hook on the ceiling of the kitchen parlor. It dangles there for a moment until Harry slits its throat. Then he cuts the body into pieces.

I don't think the Nazis would kill people that way. You should see all that blood. It makes a horrible mess!

I watch the butchering even though it's gruesome, because it's incredible how quickly a big, fat, grunting pig can be turned into so many of cuts of meat if everybody helps. We work as quickly as possible, because we don't want to get caught doing it. You can get shot for slaughtering at home and selling on the black market.

The biggest fun when we slaughter a pig is making sausages. We children get the guts of the pig and wash them out carefully. We put the heart, liver, and little pieces of meat that are left over into a grinder and mix it all together. Then we stuff the mix into the guts, cut them into pieces, and tie the ends for sausages.

Our big reward is the pig's bladder, which we make into a *Rommelpot*. You do that by scraping the bladder clean. Then you tie a smooth, small stick into the center of the bladder and tie the edges of the bladder around the top of an empty tin can. If you tie it really tight, you get a kind of drum with a stick sticking up from the middle.

Father says a *Rommelpot* would be "Roaring pot" in English, but it is not in the dictionary. You make the *Rommelpot* "roar" by holding the tin can in one hand, spitting into the palm of your other hand, and sliding your wet fist up and down the stick in the middle of the pot. It goes "Bosha-di-boisha-di-boisha," a squishy kind of noise, which most adults really don't like.

We actually use this instrument mainly during *Mardi Gras,* which in Brabants is called *Vastenavond,* the "Eve of the Fast." That night in spring, you go door-to-door in groups and ring the bell or knock. When people open up, you sing *Vastenavond* songs while you grind the *Rommelpot.* You grind on and on till the adults get sick of it; then they're supposed to pay you to get away from their doorway and stop the noise.

I earned my own *Rommelpot* from the last pig we slaughtered, and I've made a mask, but I'm sure my parents won't let me go along "serenading" the neighbors on *Vastenavond.* Maybe I'll just go with the Janssen kids, across the fields, to the Aartses next door. They've become very friendly, now that they know that we city people living in the Janssens' chickenhouse are okay even if we look strange.

Raids and Hiding Places

I t's still cold outside, so I'm sitting at the living room table again, drawing the things hanging on the wall next to the bedroom door. You may wonder why there's only a clock on the shelf, with a wire running from nowhere to the floor. I could tell you that the wire is the ground for our radio, but that would leave you asking, where's the radio?

Our virtual radio.

Well, I originally wanted to draw the radio also, but Father wouldn't let me. He took a look at what I was drawing, and he immediately got worried.

"Good heavens!" he said. "I didn't know I had left the radio standing out. I'll bet you are going to draw the radio next."

I nodded yes.

"Well, don't do it," Father said. "I should have put that radio away. If the police ever raid this place again, they shouldn't see this radio—they

55

shouldn't even see a picture with a radio in it. Either way, Harry could get into big trouble."

I knew what Father meant. Nobody is allowed to have a regular radio. Non-Jewish people can get a flat, ugly looking radio that has most radio stations blocked, except for stations that the Nazis control. We are Jewish and we aren't allowed to have any radio at all.

But we do! Our ugly old radio is one that hasn't been blocked, so that we can get all the stations. The best news programs we can receive are on Swiss National Radio, Radio Beromünster. Now I often wake up in the morning to the voice of an announcer who says: *"Guten Morgen. Hier ist Radio Beromünster. Hier sind die letzten Nachrichten."* (Good morning, this is *Radio Beromünster*. Here is the latest news.)

Police try to trace illegal radios, so I totally understand why Father wouldn't let me draw ours. He put it into its hiding place, which was built into the ceiling of the chickenhouse. And I took our alarm clock out of the bedroom and put it on the shelf to finish my picture.

We have hiding places for all our personal stuff, but we hide our other things only when we expect a raid. The police have made several raids in the neighborhood to search for Jews and Resistance members.

Fortunately, Harry gets warned about raids ahead of time by Gerrit van der Heurik, the local *Veldwachter,* or "Constable," who is one of his friends. Supposedly, nobody else in the police knows that we get these warnings.

One particular raid was especially scary. It came on December 5 a year ago. I remember the exact date because that night is Saint Nicholas Eve. We were just getting ready for a big party on the next day, Saint Nicholas Day, when Marinus Geven, another friend of Harry's, came storming into our place. The constable had said that a raid was planned that evening aimed at the Janssen farm. Since previous raids had covered all the houses in the neighborhood, someone must have told the Nazis that the Janssens were sheltering Jews.

We had to change fast from holiday preparations to getting ready for the raid. Very quickly, everything that looked like it came from the city had to disappear. I remember what happened to my things. My toothbrush and toothpaste were put behind a loose brick in the stable. My bed was taken apart, and the parts were mixed into a trash pile.

At that time, we had no special hiding place prepared for ourselves. When night came, Harry walked us deep into De Peel along trails that are hardly ever used in the winter. He brought us to an abandoned barn that had some hay left in the loft.

The hay was hardly any protection against the cold. A frigid wind blew through the many openings in the barn and chilled us to the bone. I can't remember ever being colder than I was that night.

Meanwhile, we had plenty to worry about. What would happen to us if Harry never came back? That was a serious worry because of what happened when we had been in a similar situation with the Heemert family in Kockengen. After the Nazis had done a raid there and had threatened the family, they immediately wanted to be rid of us. Would the Janssens react the same way? And worse things could happen. What if the raiders actually caught us hiding in this barn? What would we do then?

Father and Mother drilled me on what to do.

"If they ask you about the Janssens, act puzzled. If they take you to the Janssens, act as if you had never seen them before," Mother said.

"They may say to you, 'Tell us the truth, boy. If you tell us everything, we will not hurt you or your parents.' Don't believe such promises. They would never keep their word," Father said.

"And remember to use our new names," added Jan Bergsma (whom we mostly still call Heinz). "It would make it harder for the Nazis to trace us with those names, even though we still don't have our new identification cards."

At 1 a.m., Harry came back to say the raid was over.

"Where do we go now?" Father interrupted when Harry started to tell about the raid. "We're going home, of course," Harry said simply. And that is where he took us. We warmed up in the kitchen parlor and talked the rest of the night because we were so cold and upset. We also had no place to sleep because our furniture still was hidden away.

That frightful night happened last winter, but I'm reminded of it today, July 4, 1944, as I'm sitting beside the Main House, drawing our air-raid shelter across the yard. As you can see, Harry still hasn't completed building it. One of the beams is still waiting to be put inside. Many of the straw bales meant to cushion a hit from a bomb still need to be plastered with peat and mud.

Air-raid shelters are fairly common on the farms around here. If a bomb hits right on top of you, a shelter won't do much for you, but if there is shrapnel flying around, it can give you some good protection.

Our half-finished air raid shelter

When Harry started to build the shelter, however, he thought of it more as a place where he could fit in a secret room for us to hide if the Nazis made another raid looking for Jews. Hard as he tried, it didn't work. You could still tell from the outside that there was something extra built into the inside. That's probably why Harry will never finish the shelter.

Instead, he thought it might work to build a good hiding place for us in the stable. He had a bricklayer build two walls between the cow stalls and the horse stall. From the outside, it looks like there's only a single wall because the space between the two walls is so narrow. To get in or out, we have to climb up into the rafters and then be let down into the narrow space between the walls.

We used it once during a raid. It was an awful experience. We dangled for a long time from a rope in the rafters while they lowered us ever so slowly and carefully, so that we wouldn't scrape ourselves against the bricks on the way down. Once we hit the floor, we had very little space to stand in. There wasn't any room even to tum around.

No one had thought to put a potty in the hiding place. Soon, the place stank so terribly that it was no longer a secret that people were hiding there. Fortunately, no Nazis came into the stable to look for us. But I'll never forget that awful smell.

Sick in Bed

Father was sick in bed last week, and he drew a cartoon of how sick he was to get some sympathy from his friend Frans back in Amsterdam. In the picture, you can see our makeshift nightstand with home-made medicine on it. Father got better without any doctor.

Mother in wooden shoes by Father's bedside.

When Mother got sick a while later, home remedies didn't help. Harry said that there was a doctor in town, but he wasn't sure the man could be trusted with the secret that his patient was Jewish.

The adults discussed the risk, and I hung in the doorway between the bedroom and the living room, listening in.

"Well, I can have a look at this doctor's handwriting," Heinz offered and explained that back in Amsterdam, he had tracked criminals by examining the letters they wrote.

So Harry said, "Nothing ventured, nothing gained! I'll try to get a note that doctor wrote to a patient, and let's see what you can make out from it."

Harry found one soon enough. Heinz studied it a while, and then he gave a lively description of what the man was like.

"That's amazing," Harry said. "It's like you know him in person!"

"Yes," Heinz said, "and going by his handwriting, I wouldn't trust him."

"Okay," Harry said. "That agrees with my own hunch. There isn't much choice though. The only other doctor that works our neighborhood is Hendrik Wiegersma, and he's kind of unusual. He sounds like a quack, but people here love him, and I think he's absolutely trustworthy. He makes no secret about what he thinks of the Nazis."

Father told me later what a *quack* is. It means a doctor who has his own personal methods for treating sick people. Then Father said again to stop listening in when adults are talking among themselves.

In the end, they decided to have Dr. Wiegersma come, and I was excited to meet him because of his reputation as a real character. Zus, Nel, and I stood at the big window of the Graumanns' bedroom to watch him come. Actually, we could hear him before we even saw him. He rode a motorcycle without mufflers, and he came roaring toward our farm, throwing up a big cloud of dust on our dirt road.

He skidded into the yard, tossed his helmet to Riek, and grabbed his black bag from the luggage rack. He strode to the house on tall black boots, and the minute he got through the door he started screaming.

"Where is that nut from the city that doesn't know enough to keep herself from getting sick?" he yelled.

He is a rough-talking man, but he seems to be a good doctor. Mother got better fast on the medicine he told her to take.

My Mother's Day Present

Today is May 8, 1944, and soon it'll be Mother's Day. I already have made her a present, a calendar decorated with *zilver papier.* We call it "silver paper" even though it really is aluminum foil backed with black paper. The strips come in handy for art projects. If you weave the white aluminum side in one direction and the black reverse side in the other direction, you get a nice pattern.

We love the silver paper because it comes from America, and it is dropped here by the American planes that fly by almost every day. We can see them clearly during daylight, and we can hear them drone past even at night. They are on their way to bomb Germany.

Calendar with "zilver papier"

The Nazi Germans want to shoot the American planes down, and they use radar to pinpoint the position of the planes. To confuse the radar, the American airmen toss out silver paper. This doesn't always work; far too often the American planes still are hit.

Nel, Zus and I have collected quite a bit of silver paper, but don't get the idea that we can just scoop it up from the fields. Even though the planes drop it in bunches, by the time it flutters down to the ground, it is spread pretty far and wide. Nel and Zus sing a little prayer to Saint Anthony that's supposed to help you find stuff: *Heilige Antonius, beste vrind, maak dat'k een papiertje vind.* ("Holy Anthony, good and kind, what I lost, please help me find.") The prayer works. The day I started using it, I collected a whole bagful of silver paper.

When Nazi guns hit American planes, the American airmen parachute out to save their lives. Not long ago, a pilot landed near here; neighbors took him in and sent for help to get him back home.

The pilot, however, couldn't tell Dutch from German and he couldn't grasp that he was in friendly hands rather than about to be imprisoned. He was so upset that the neighbors brought him to our place to reassure him. They knew that Father speaks good English, and indeed, Father was able to quickly calm him down. The two of them got along so well that they talked the whole night long.

Tinus-Oom's Peaches

I t's June 2, 1944, and it's getting to be more like summer today. I am sitting beside our sunny corner, sketching our little orchard as I view it through the unfinished barn. You can see the posts of where the walls are going to be, with the sun shining lighting up the fruit trees on the other side. Our orchard has apples, pears, and peaches. Even though our own peaches aren't ripe yet, we have already harvested peaches from *Tinus-Oom's* orchard in 't Derp. We call him "Uncle Tinus" because he is Dina's uncle. He moved in with the Janssens some years ago because he was getting too old to live by himself.

View of our little orchard.

Since he no longer lives near his orchard, there's no one to watch it. Last year, thieves stole all the peaches several days before we came to pick them. So this year, we went over there early and picked the peaches half-ripe—before anyone would think to steal them.

By "we" I don't mean me. I still have to stay in or near the chickenhouse all the time while the other kids get to do fun things like picking peaches in 't Derp.

The Janssens put a big barrel of Tinus-Oom's half-ripe peaches at the side entrance to the Main House. I'm always hungry, so every time I go in or out, I take a peach. Now I have a bad tummy-ache. Mother says that will teach me not to stuff myself like a pig.

Speaking of Tinus-Oom, he has lately caused us a lot of worry. Before we came to the Janssen farm, he was living in Harry's empty chickenhouse. Since Harry had no other place to put us, he gave us Tinus-Oom's place to live in and moved him behind the kitchen parlor into a dark room that they had used as a pantry. He didn't like that at all.

That's the reason Tinus-Oom was angry with us from the moment we came. Recently, he has started to act really crazy, yelling that he wanted us gone. A few days ago, he even threatened to call the police.

Harry thought the old man would be all right again if we just left him alone. But Heinz said he believed Tinus-Oom would really go to the police. He convinced Harry that Tinus-Oom was a threat to all of us and that he would have to be taken away.

So Tinus-Oom had to go to a sanitarium. Crotchety as he was, I was sorry to see him go. He belonged to the farm, and not having him there made the place less like home.

He died a few weeks later. I guess he missed us, too. No one really told me he died. I just picked up the news in passing from Nel when she and I were recovering from being kicked by some miserable sheep.

That thing started out looking like fun. The sheep had pulled up the pegs to which they were chained, and they had run off to the Aartses next door, where the grass looked greener.

Nel and I volunteered to get them home. We circled behind them and then let go with a real whoopee, like cowboys. The sheep responded by trotting off fast with the pegs on their chains going clickety-clack after them. Stubborn as they were, they ran in the wrong direction.

"We'd better pull them back by their chains before they get too far," I said. I ran off after the first one, caught up, and meant to stop it by stomping my foot on the peg. The sheep didn't stop and I fell on my nose.

Nel did better, grabbed a chain, and held on tight. Both sheep stopped then, so I got up and grabbed the other chain, and we started pulling. "Go, sheep, go-o-o-o," we yelled.

Go they did—in circles. We held on tight as we spun around like tops till the sheep had enough—and stopped absolutely dead.

"Haul them in," Nel said. So we went hand over hand along their chains till we had them by the collar strap. But no matter how we yanked on the strap or kicked the stupid sheep, they wouldn't move, and they kicked us back hard.

That hurt, so we gave up, but we were too embarrassed to show up at home without the sheep. We let the sheep go, and they went on peacefully grazing on the Aartses' meadow. Pretty soon the sun went down, and the sheep ran off on their own to go to their stalls.

We went running after them, doing our best to whoop and holler to make it seem we were chasing them in.

Nobody was fooled, however, and we still got a ribbing.

Then Harry got serious. "I know you kids were trying hard," he said. "Let me show you how you move a sheep with ease".

Father went with us. Harry stepped behind

Sheep looking like a devil

a sheep. Quickly he grabbed a hind leg, started walking, and the sheep meekly hopped beside him on its other three legs.

"Simple as pie," Harry said.

"Good lesson," Father said. That evening he made me a cartoon with a poem that said, "Don't let any sheep bedevil you."

Harry's Favorite Businesses

It's July 2, 1944. It's really nice weather today, so I am sitting outside the barn, drawing Harry's tractor. He is getting ready to take it out on the road to do threshing, which separates kernels of wheat or rye from the plant once it is ripe.

Harry gets all the threshing business in the neighborhood because he's the only one around here who has a tractor and mechanical thresher. The work will start really soon.

Harry's tractor, ready for threshing.

Harry is especially proud of his threshing business. He sits straight on his tractor seat as he pulls his threshing rig from one farm to the next. If a stranger asks what he does for a living, Harry says: "threshing contractor."

I remember the threshing routine from last year. First, Harry loops a long belt around the big flywheel in the middle of the tractor and runs it to the drive wheel of the threshing machine. Then he runs another belt to the chaff blower, driven by a small electric motor on the side of the tractor behind the steering wheel. Then the noisy, dusty job begins. It's lots of fun to watch, but I have to cover my nose.

Harry tending his bee hives.

Harry is just as proud of his beekeeping skills. He doesn't earn much money from his bees; instead, he gets lots of respect from the neighborhood for the way he handles bees. He can stride up to a beehive, often even without any protection. Other times he wears just a face mask. He knows just when bees become easily angered. That's when he dresses up with protection from head to toe to keep from getting stung.

People look to Harry whenever a bee swarm settles down in their area. The minute Harry hears about it, he goes into action. He calms the swarm down, drops the ball of bees into an empty hive, and takes the whole thing home. He expands his bee business without putting out any money. At the same time, he gets lots of thanks from his bee-panicked neighbors.

Birthday and Anniversary Cards

The Janssens have been noticing all along that we like birthday cards with poems. Annie was the first one to show she was interested, and she was a bit shy about asking to make her one. She just hung around, taking a quick look now and then, while Father was helping me with a poem for a card I was preparing for Mother.

March 1943

Geliefde Moes, Uweet, dat knopen
Op 't ogenblik niet zijn te kopen
Ik kreeg niets anders dan die scheven
En hoop U zult er niets om geven
Ook zijn, helaas, zij iets wat duur
Maar ik, ik keek daarom niet zuur
Het deert mij, Moesje, evenmin
Zit in mijn portemonnaie niets in.
Tot slot neem hier die dikke woen,
'k Beloof U, steeds mijn best te doen.

The poem reads, "I'm giving Mother used buttons for her birthday."

"You want something, Zus?" Father asked her after a while.

"I, eh, w-want something for our f-father," she said. "Maybe a drawing. Could you make me one?"

71

"It wouldn't have to be right away," she added quickly. "We could make it for his birthday. It doesn't come till January."

"Certainly, I'll be glad to make you a drawing," Father answered. "What would you like me to put in the picture?"

She couldn't say, so Father made her a colorful bouquet of flowers. She liked it. "Would you like a poem with it?" Father asked then.

"What is a poem?" Annie asked back.

"It's a song without music," Father said.

Father put together a few verses and showed her how rhythm and rhyme make a poem. Then he made the drawing and the verse into a birthday card.

Annie got really excited about it. Sunday evening after supper, she came up behind her father with a smile and little giggle. Suddenly, she pulled her hand holding the birthday card from behind her back, stuck it in her father's face, and said quickly, "Here, this is for you."

"That's great, thank you," Harry said. "That's a really beautiful birthday card, but it won't be my birthday for another six months."

"I know," said Annie, "but it's too long to wait."

Harry also had an idea for a card. He wanted it for Friedus and Trineke van Schayk, the parents-in-law of Harry's brother Thy. They are the favorite couple of old people in the neighborhood, and they were about to celebrate their 50th Wedding Anniversary. Harry loves them as if they were his own parents, and he started organizing the neighborhood to make a bang-up party for them. So he wanted Father to make a Happy Anniversary card for the occasion.

"Is this going to be a safe group of people?" Father asked Harry. "I imagine folks will start asking where you got a hand-made card around here if the van Schayks start showing it around."

"Perfectly safe," Harry said. "I'm inviting only old friends that can be trusted completely, so we can relax and have a good time."

"In that case," Father said, "how about we prepare a skit?"

"You mean, a show, just for Friedus and Trineke?" Harry asked.

"Yes. We'll ask people to tell us things about Friedus and Trineke that we can use to gently poke fun at them."

"That's great. I know a few good stories about them that we can use," Harry said.

"Maybe I'll even toss a few lines to make fun of the Nazi Occupation," Father said.

I was amazed that Father could think up something funny about the Nazis who have been turning our lives completely upside down. But in the end, we all had a great time with this skit. It had a part for each person in the Janssen family, including the children. I didn't get a part because they decided that we refugees still shouldn't take the risk of appearing in a crowd. We were present, however, at the rehearsals that went on every day for more than two weeks.

The whole neighborhood got caught up in trying give the van Schayks the greatest anniversary party ever. They even built them an *ereboog*, "a gate of honor." It was made of peat briquettes and decorated with electric bulbs that beamed festively into the dark night.

A gate of honor for the van Schayks.

When Harry took us to see it the night before the party, he was all excited. He told us that there are stories from long ago about people honored with an *ereboog*, but he hadn't seen one since he was a young boy.

Nazis Raid the *Joodse Invalide*

Not long after the party for the van Schayks, our joyful mood turned into deep grief.

Little Jo came out back to the Chickenhouse to say a tall, blonde woman from the city was at the Main House and asked for my parents. We figured it must be Ans Burbach, my parents' good friend because she and her husband Frans are the only people in Amsterdam who know where we are. Even though they have kept in touch with us, they came only once before to visit us in person.

We were surprised at the visit, and we would have been overjoyed to see Ans, except that her coming like this unannounced could only mean trouble. Something really awful must have happened.

Nazis loading people onto a truck.

We didn't have long to wait before she told us: "It's about Jacob."

Jacob is my Opa. "Oh, God," I prayed quietly. "Please don't let the bad news be about Opa. I need him to be there when I get back to Amsterdam."

While I was saying this to myself, Ans went on talking.

"I heard from my neighbors that the Nazis were raiding the *Joodse Invalide*," she said. "I jumped on my bicycle and raced over to see what was happening. By the time I arrived, the Nazis had loaded all the old people on trucks. I couldn't even say goodbye to Jacob."

Ans and Mother cried together. "I'll never be able to smile again," Mother said.

"You'll be surprised," Father answered. "Life goes on. You'll see. You'll even laugh again."

I didn't cry then. I waited until I was alone in bed. Much later, I saw a picture of how the Nazis loaded people on trucks like they did Opa. Then I cried again.

Starting My Jewish Studies

Father added Jewish Studies to my home school lessons, and the idea for it came from another Jewish man who is hiding in our neighborhood. We're not supposed to know where he is hiding or what his name is. It's safer that way.

We do know that he had been studying to be a rabbi before the Nazis closed his school. Since we don't know his name, we call him *De Onder Rabbijn,* roughly, "Rabbi Under Study."

De Onder Rabbijn told us he is writing a book. No big surprise to me. Writing is a good way to pass the time when you can't get out of the house. We all do it. The student-rabbi's topic is a textbook on Jewish Studies for kids about my age. Father is working on a guidebook for people who want to get more out of going to art museums. Heinz is writing a play on the life of Moliere, a Frenchman who himself is famous for the plays he wrote.

The student-rabbi asked Father to review his writing and suggest changes. Father agreed, and they decided to have Father teach the lessons and see what worked for me and what didn't.

Now, we get weekly lessons sent to us in a notebook titled *Brieven aan een Jonge Vriend* ("Letters to a Young Friend.") Every chapter has a section on the Hebrew language, Jewish history, and Bible stories. I particularly like the Bible stories, and I've started to make drawings of them.

Father looked at the drawing I made of Balaam and the talking donkey. "Interesting lesson in that story," he said. "Here we have a man who can't

Angels trying to set Balaam straight.

77

see that he's on the wrong path even though an angel is stopping him and his donkey refuses to move along."

"Yes," I said, "Can you see that in my picture there's another angel who's coming to help out?"

"Good idea," Father said. "You and me might be a little like Balaam; maybe we don't appreciate angels enough who are looking out for us."

I felt pretty good that day, but often I feel more like Jonah in the story of Jonah and the Whale. Like me, Jonah had to leave his comfortable home and lost his former neighbors and friends. Like me, he got sent unexpectedly to a strange country. He had to travel part way in the belly of a big fish, and that made me think of how we were supposed to be traveling to safety in the belly of a big gasoline truck. Jonah got dumped in Nineveh and I in Brabant. He and I both landed with people who talk a strange language and dress in a different way.

So I drew a picture of the whale spitting up Jonah on a beach outside Nineveh. You can see the town and the harbor in the background. Jonah said his trip made no sense to him and my trip to Brabant makes little sense to me; sometimes I want to go sit under a carob tree and cry, like he did.

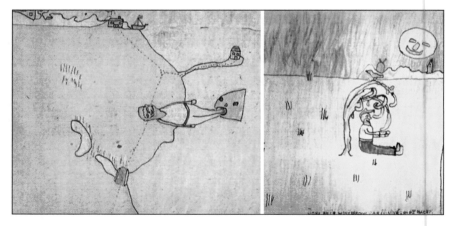

Jonah landing in Nineveh.   Jonah under a carob tree at night.

Seeing the War Up Close

The war is coming close to us these days, so that we don't have to use maps to spot the battles anymore. It's one thing to see battles on a map. It's another thing to see people who get killed or wounded in these battles. There is too much killing, and there's got to be another way to solve problems.

It made me think of the Bible story of the fight between David and Goliath. The Jewish army and the Philistine army were going for a fight. Then David stepped up and settled the matter one-on-one with Goliath.

David facing Goliath with the Jewish Army in the background.

A Jewish champion ought to go to Berlin and face up to Hitler. With a single stone, or perhaps in this case, with a well-aimed bullet, all the misery in the world would come to an end.

Of course, at the end of the Goliath story, the enemy dies; in our case, an enemy soldier turned up merely wounded right in our kitchen parlor. Harry and his friend Marinus Geven found him and two other German soldiers wandering in a daze along a path in *De Peel.*

We kids trooped to the kitchen parlor to see the soldiers. Allied troops are pushing the Nazis away, so we're no longer so worried about searches on our farm.

Marinus is a medic. He told the soldiers that if they would surrender their weapons, he would treat the wounded man and find a place for all of them to hide until the Americans arrived. The soldiers nodded in agreement.

While Marinus dressed the wounds, one of the other men talked. He didn't have much military information. He was just a small farmer from across the border who got drafted into the German Army. His crops are ruined and his family is starving because there's no one at home to tend his farm.

The wound Marinus was working on was amazing to see—a shot straight through the neck. Marinus said it was a miracle that it didn't kill him. He was bleeding, but he could breathe and swallow.

As Marinus was finishing his treatment, a Nazi lieutenant burst into our kitchen parlor and barked at the three soldiers for hanging out with civilians. Then he raised his gun and marched them out of the house ahead of him. Fortunately, he ignored the rest of us—and they were gone!

I know what happened to the man who was shot through the neck. Jan Janssen found him two days later, dead in a ditch nearby. Marinus said that it was a pity he hadn't been able to treat the man further. If only he had stayed, he wouldn't be dead now.

I also have been coming across dead bodies in ditches along the road. To me, they are a dreadful sight, but Jan Janssen doesn't spend any time feeling sorry for them—he rolls them, meaning that he grabs anything he likes from the bodies. He gets maps, cigarettes, rifles, bullets —even boots that he pulls right off the dead man's legs.

"The Axis Is Broken"

On September 24, 1944, we heard the fighting come even closer. People around here say, "The Axis is Broken." Father explained what that means. When the Germans and the Italians were united in fighting the Allies, they called themselves "the Axis." It's another way of saying "axle," and it means that they saw themselves as the axle of two wheels rolling them to victory.

Well, now they are losing, and Father has predicted for a while that Allied armies will liberate us by September 28, his birthday. When Harry heard that, he thought it might take a bit longer. Father stuck by his prediction, so Harry said, "Let's bet on it."

Father said, "Let's make it a guilder." Father's not one for making big bets!

Harry said: "Whatever you like. Either way, I'll win. If I lose the guilder, I'll get freedom sooner!"

Well, Father won his bet. We heard artillery firing in spurts all during the night, and we hardly slept. Early in the morning, Harry jumped on his bike to go see what was happening.

He came back after breakfast and said that Nazi soldiers were running away on horse carts and bicycles. Their tanks, it seemed, had run out of gas.

Father decided we should all go take a look at the soldiers who were coming to liberate us.

"Isn't it dangerous to go that close to the fighting?" I asked.

"Yes it is," Father answered. "Everything we do is dangerous. To me it's worth the risk to see our liberators with my own eyes. But I wouldn't blame you one bit if you want to stay here on the farm while Mother and I go to the *Harde Weg*."

Of course, I decided to go along to the *Harde Weg*. In Dutch, that means "the Paved Road," our nickname for the main road that runs

81

through *De Voorpeel* because it is the only road in the neighborhood that has a hard surface.

It's been raining practically every day, and all the dirt roads are flooded. So we had to slush through the mud—not too much fun. People had laid logs on the foot path as a kind-of bridge across the worst mud puddles. You had to walk carefully because the logs were slippery from all the rain; if you slipped off, you got soaking wet.

The Allied tanks on the *Harde Weg* were moving slowly, single file, when we first saw them. They weren't able to go anywhere where it wasn't paved. They're so big, they'd get stuck for sure. The tanks slowed and stopped as we got closer.

Father jumped on one of the tank treads to get close to the soldier inside and yelled: "Thank you, we've been waiting for you a long time." He had to yell really loud to be heard above the roar of the idling tank engine.

"Get down. Quick. Into a foxhole," the soldier yelled back. "They're firing on us." And he ducked down into the turret of the tank.

Father, Mother, and I each jumped down into one of the foxholes. The moment I dropped inside the hole, water started bubbling into my wooden shoes and seeping up my pants legs. It felt icy. Then a volley of shots hit the paved road. I could see the bullets splash into the dirt. They left little craters.

That was scary enough. But then, all of a sudden, there was this ter- rific boom, and a haystack in the field beside me flared yellow and red. Pieces of burning hay were flying everywhere. Boy, that really scared me! When the firing stopped for a bit, I reached down for my wooden shoes, jumped out of the hole, and ran home through the mud with the wooden shoes in my hands.

Father and Mother stayed behind. I don't know whether Father was able to talk any more with the British soldiers. I doubt he was able to say or hear more than a few words between all that shooting.

The Scottish Army Camp

Today, October 15, 1944, is my birthday. I'm celebrating it with a troop of Scottish soldiers who pitched their tents at the end of our street, the *Voorpeelweg*. They came last week, and as soon as I could get away, I went to see what was going on.

Nowadays, I go down the road barefoot. There is no point wearing my wooden shoes anymore because the mud on the footpath is so sticky, it pulls the shoes right off my feet.

The flooding and the mud are worse now because the Allies run their tanks right across the fields to chase the Nazis. They use light tanks so they don't sink in, but they're heavy enough to crush our drainage tiles. The water just stands, and it has been very wet here this fall to begin with.

When I got to the Scottish Army camp the first time, the soldiers were surprised to see me. No one else from the neighborhood had come to visit them. Me, I was relieved to be able to get away from the chickenhouse. I had been cooped up too long.

"Who you?" a soldier asked me and pointed at my chest.

"You don't need to talk to me in sign language," I answered. "I speak English. My Father has been teaching it to me for two years, now."

"Can you imagine?" the Scottish soldier said to no one in particular. "This farm lad speaks English."

I explained that I originally was from the city and not strictly a "farm lad," but this hardly registered. The soldier started presenting me to everyone in his camp as a farm lad who speaks English. They were excited to hear what I could tell them about our neighborhood. Especially about which farms had girls they could visit.

One of the Scottish soldiers, Charlie Fraser, has taken a special interest in me. He couldn't pronounce my name Frans when he met me, so he called me "Frankie," and all the other men in the company started doing the same. He also calls me "Pal." He wants to know all about my family, and when I told him how we were living in a chickenhouse with the Janssens, he said he'd like to come to visit.

I guess compared to a tent in a sea of mud, our chickenhouse on a dry farmyard seems like an improvement. Anyway, Charlie likes it. He keeps coming home with me, and each time he asks if he can bring something. I had been eyeing the company's small ammunition boxes, figuring one of them would make a great lunch box. I told him I'd like one.

The next evening, after dark, Charlie was back, knocking on the chickenhouse door. When we started to close the door behind him, he said, "Wait, I have your ammunition box outside."

I wondered why he hadn't brought it in with him, but I found out quick when I stepped outside with him. He pointed to a large metal container, as big as a seaman's trunk.

"There's your ammunition box, Pal," he said. "I had a devil of a time lugging it here through the mud."

I didn't have the heart

Charlie's sizable ammunition box.

to tell him that this trunk-sized box is not what I had wanted. I kept it to store my clothes in, and my clothes have stayed amazingly dry, even in all this wet weather.

"Can I do something for you, lad?" Charlie said again when I visited the Scottish company this morning.

"Nice of you to ask," I replied. "Today's my birthday."

"Oh, we should be giving you something very special. How old might you be now?"

"Eleven," I said.

"Something special for a big lad," Charlie said. "What could it be?" Just then there was a loud boom of a cannon going off. "Don't worry, Frankie," Charlie said. "It's just a message for the Jerries to head them back to Germany." He often called the German soldiers "Jerries."

"You're going to be firing more shots?" I asked. Charlie nodded, yes. "Well, then," I said. "May I fire the next round? I want to send my own message to the Jerries."

"I'll ask the Lieutenant," Charlie said.

Lieutenant Morris was one of my friends. "Don't ever tell anybody I said it was all right," he told Charlie. "I'll be looking elsewhere when Frankie pulls the release."

The Scottish army cap, fixed to fit me.

The Scottish soldiers loaded the cannon and all I had to do was to give the release a little yank. But the recoil and mighty boom that resulted made me feel tremendously happy.

As a memento, the soldiers gave me this cap of theirs. I can't wear it right away because, naturally, it is too big for my head. One of the soldiers who is handy with needle and thread says he'll cut the end off the cap and then sew it back together smaller. Even Jan Janssen will be impressed.

We Say Goodbye to De Peel

I stayed in Brabant almost a year after we were liberated because the Nazis kept fighting to come back. By early May, when the Nazis finally let go of the rest of Holland, they had stolen all of the food.

Thank God, we have enough food on the farm, and it doesn't make sense for us to go back to Amsterdam and be hungry there. We heard that people were eating tulip bulbs. They were even eating them *raw.* They couldn't cook what little food they had because they had no wood to heat their stoves.

Father went anyway because he wanted to help friends who were starving. For his trip, Father packed peas, beans, and potatoes into a crate. He arranged to get a ride on a truck going north, and he hasn't come back. Mother says he got sick on the way and landed in a hospital in Barneveld. She says that when we go up North, I can't even go to visit Father, even though Barneveld is right along the road to Amsterdam.

Mother also made a trip to Amsterdam to see how things looked up North. She went to our old apartment and found that another family is living there. The neighbors said these new tenants were Nazi lovers, so Mother went to the police to have them thrown out.

It doesn't look like the police will act anytime soon. Even if eventually we get the apartment back, we wouldn't have any furniture because the Nazis stole it all. So Mother made arrangements for us to move in with her friends, Ans and Frans Burbach.

When Mother and I finally left *De Peel* together, it was hard to say goodbye to the Janssens. They are our good friends—besides being the people who saved our lives. After we finished hugging them goodbye, we went to say more goodbyes to the neighbors, who also are our friends.

I am painting a picture of us walking up the lane from the Manders' farm, which is next to the Janssens. In the picture, Hanna Manders and her brother Marinus are waving goodbye. I am carrying my wooden doll, Friedje, with me in my backpack as a souvenir. The rest of our things already have been sent ahead to Amsterdam.

Waving a sad goodbye.

Mother put an advertisement in the local newspaper to thank everybody in the neighborhood. We didn't have the chance to come by in person to say thanks and goodbye to everyone we know. Actually, we found out that most people in *De Voorpeel* knew we were hiding with the Janssens, and they helped protect us by keeping their mouth shut.

When we got back to Amsterdam, going back to regular school felt good, but then, late that summer, mother dropped a bomb. Out of a clear blue sky, she said: "Max, your father is dead. He died three months ago."

I interrupted: "What! Three months ago, and all that time, you didn't tell me?"

Mother looked pale. Lamely she said, "Well, you know, you weren't feeling all that well, and I didn't want to upset you."

I didn't criticize her any further. I was really feeling rotten, and I knew she wasn't feeling any better. Besides that, I could have asked the grownups more questions about what was going on with Father. All summer long, they kept saying he was in the hospital. Something was fishy about that. Why didn't any of us visit him there?

I decided that mainly none of us wanted to deal with any more bad news. I didn't want to ask about Father, and they didn't want to tell. Still, I think that adults are crazy if they think that kids can't tell when they're not being told the truth about what's going on around them.

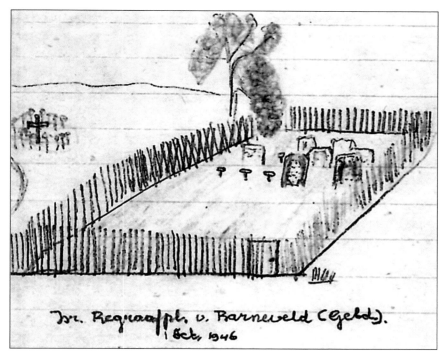

Jr. Begraafpl. v. Barneveld (Geld).
1 Oct, 1946

Father's grave in Barneveld.

I actually didn't see Father's grave until October 1, 1946, when I sat in the Jewish section of the cemetery of Barneveld, drawing the place. Father died the previous June, and if he were still alive, he would be 46 years old now.

The last time I saw Father alive was in May of last year, when he decided to try to go to Amsterdam even though at the time it wasn't really safe. Nazis were still running around with guns because the war wasn't completely over. I can still picture him, waving goodbye from the cab of the truck that was taking him North.

A few days after he left, I got very sick. My skin turned yellow, and I had a high fever. Dr. Wiegersma was really worried, and he sent me to the regional hospital in Eindhoven. Father and I had been swimming in the big canal in *De Peel,* and Dr. Wiegersma thought maybe we'd both caught typhus, a dangerous disease that is very catching.

So they put me in the hospital in a glass cage with just a bed and a nightstand. I felt so bad, I didn't even realize where they were putting me. They gave me meals by pushing trays through a small window in the glass.

At first, I could hardly eat. Then, one morning, I suddenly felt much better. My skin was normal pink again, and I had a good appetite.

I was bored out of my mind alone in that glass cage, so I took red paint from a set of watercolor paints I had with me, and I painted my face red. I meant to be funny, but the nurses didn't get it and thought I was getting seriously sick. Boy, were they mad when they found out what I had done!

The only person I knew who visited me was Elli, Heinz's wife. She had come to Eindhoven to keep me company, and she stayed on. She lived in a hotel near the hospital.

Nobody told me why Mother didn't come to see me. I now know that she couldn't because she had to go to Father's funeral. At the time, however, Elli didn't say anything about that. I was scared and worried because I didn't know what either my Mother or my Father was doing and why they left me here by myself in this glass cage in the hospital.

It took a couple of weeks, but finally the doctors got test results that showed I didn't have typhus, and Elli took me home to the chicken-house. That was long before we moved back to Amsterdam.

Visiting My Grandmother

It's June 10, 1946, and I am sitting in the backyard of my grand-mother's house in England, where Mother and I came to visit. Grandma Dina Heppner is my father's mother, and she lives near London.

I'm drawing the backside of grandmother's house, where I can see her through the kitchen window. She is cooking supper for the family, which includes my Aunt Dorothy and her son, Stephan.

Grandmother's house.

I was only four when we visited here last, but I remember *Oma Dinchen* clearly, especially her soft padded hands. She used to move them in time with a song while she played a hand game. I even remember the words: *"Lass deine Händchen drehen, dass es eine Lust ist anzusehen.* (It's fun to spin your hands and watch them move.)

She is just as soft and sweet today as she was then. Right now, she is making buttered mashed spinach by hand just the way Father and I always liked it.

Aunt Dorothy and Cousin Stephan have trouble knowing what to do with me. I'm no longer the baby they remember from before the war, and they see me as different in some way because I spent the war running and hiding from the Nazis.

I ruined it with Stephen when I told Aunt Dorothy how the Nazis stole my bike. Right away, she wanted to buy me another one. But there were no bikes to be had—new or used—even in England.

So my aunt said to Stephan: "You give your bike to Cousin Max because he hasn't had one all this time. I'll buy you another one when bikes can be had again."

Stephan said, "All right," but he didn't mean it. I think he went along with his mother because all of them felt guilty around me.

I said, "Thanks so much, Steve."

He said gruffly, "You'll call me Stephan. That's my name, you understand?" And he pushed the bicycle at me so hard, it almost crashed into me.

I should have said, "Keep it." Now, Stephan is angry, but it's too late to try to make things right. They've already packed up the bike and shipped it to Holland.

Back in Amsterdam

It's September 15, 1946, and I am back in the apartment house of Ans and Frans Burbach in Amsterdam. Their street, the *Westland Gracht,* is on the west side of town. A *gracht is* a city canal that runs down the middle of the street, except this *gracht* has houses on only one side of the canal

The room I sleep in was a storage room in the attic before I came. In fact, it looks much like the attic room where Father hid in our old apartment house on the south side of town when the Nazis raided it three years ago.

In the house where we lived then, it was dangerous to climb out on the roof, but here it's common for people to do so. There is a graveled area on the roof with some benches where people can sit in the sun.

It's overcast today. I have the roof to myself, so I can do some sketching and some thinking. I'm looking across the *gracht* where there is open farmland with a lot of greenhouses. That's what I'm putting in the picture that I'm working on.

The Burbachs gave Mother their bedroom to use; they sleep on day-beds in the sitting room and dining room. Mother has gotten back some things that people saved for us, and you can see them in her room, for example, the silver bowl on the cabinet and the big painting on the wall.

Lately, Mother has been spending most of the day in her room with the door shut. When I ask her how she feels, she just cries and says she doesn't know what to do. I think that, in fact, she *does* know what to do, she just doesn't want to discuss it. She wants to move to America.

I hate that idea, but I know her reasons: Here in Holland, we have no money, no home, no furniture, no work. Mother wants me and her to go live with my Aunt Helen and her husband, Uncle Max. They moved to America just before the Nazis came to Holland. They have a place for us to live, and they can tell Mother what to do when she feels so desperate. Still, I don't like it.

I hate the idea because my old geography book, which was shipped back from *De Voorpeel,* says that America is a country with wild Indians in the West and Gangsters in Chicago. Aunt Helen and Uncle Max don't live in the West or in Chicago. They live in Cleveland, but it's the same country and besides, they say they'll get me a job selling newspapers.

View from the Burbachs' roof (above); Mother's bedroom (below).

HET MEISJE MET DE ZWAVELSTOKJES

The poor little match girl from my story book.

I hate that idea the worst of all. The only people I've ever heard of selling newspapers for a living are beggars and poor orphans, like the poor little match girl in my Hans Christian Anderson story book. I want to stay in the school I just started here in Holland; I'm just barely starting to make friends in my new class.

I am just sitting here, thinking about all this trouble, and then I just go back inside through the attic window without even finishing my drawing.

I think Mother understood how bad I felt. Before we left Holland, she arranged a trip back to *De Peel*, which is so familiar to me.

It's doubly good that we went because, soon afterwards, they had a fire on the Janssen farm, and the whole place burned to the ground. The fire started in the haystack, where Little Jo and Martin were playing with matches. They played in the haystack often, and they'd been told over and over to keep their hands off the matches, but it didn't help. I still have a picture I drew of them long ago sitting on a haystack. None of the buildings I drew are left, except for the pig sty. The chickenhouse, my home for so long, is gone. Even the unfinished air raid

Two little boys on the haystack.

shelter and the partially built new barn are ashes; now Harry doesn't have to worry anymore about finishing the construction.

Fortunately I have a copy of a painting that Heinz made of *De Peelbloem,* the name of the Janssen home. Heinz also made a trip there before the fire, but not Elli. She is dead.

Heinz's painting of *De Peelbloem.*

No one told me when, where, why, or how she died. People still keep dying and disappearing, like they have been ever since the Nazis came here. You can't even say goodbye to people after they die. There are no funerals.

I miss Elli even though we had our troubles. I also miss *De Peelbloem,* but Harry has decided not to rebuild it. He says he is moving the whole family to Brazil and starting over in a new country. Like us.

Traveling to America

It's November 10, 1946, and I am on the ship *Hai-Lee* that is taking us to America. I have the upper bunk in Cabin Number 8. My roommate, who sleeps below me, is a fat Belgian who smokes. Ugh.

I'm sitting on a small stool with my notebook on my lap against the far wall to draw our bunks. My sketchbook is in a big trunk in the hold, where I can't get at it, so I have to make do with this old notebook. There's little for me to do on this ship but draw.

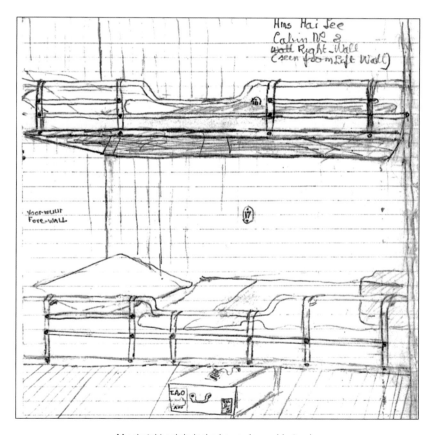

My sketchbook is locked away in our big trunk.

The *Hai-Lee* is a troop ship that the Nationalist Chinese bought from the Norwegians. It's making just this one trip across the ocean, and so they put very few things on board to entertain passengers. We all are refugees from Europe.

The weather report says there's going to be a big storm on the North Atlantic, so instead of steaming directly west toward America, we're headed south toward Africa. We'll go across on the South Atlantic, which is quieter, but the trip will take an extra week. Ugh again. Who wants to spend two weeks bunking with a fat Belgian who smokes?

Mother is luckier. She is bunking with a nice woman from Vienna in the Women's Section.

The next people to sleep in our bunks here will be Nationalist Chinese soldiers. They still have a war in China, fighting the Communists, whoever they are. Will this awful fighting ever stop?

Well, anyway, there is no war in America. No bombs, no battles. That's pretty good. I still hate the idea of going there, but now, there's no turning back.

Aunt Helen wrote that I don't *have* to sell newspapers and that anyway, many American boys my age deliver newspapers before or after school. They get regular pay, and they don't have to sit on a street comer and beg.

That sounds a little better, but I still don't want to sell newspapers and I don't want to live in a country full of strangers that don't even speak Dutch. Aunt Helen says, don't worry, I'll like it in Cleveland, where she and Uncle Max Forchheimer live. We'll see if I do.

We got to Cleveland in late November, and now it's mid-January. I can't say life here is easy. It's pretty crowded in the Forchheimer apartment. Aunt Helen and Uncle Max use one bedroom to sleep in and another one for an office. He works from home as an agent for a furniture manufacturer. Their son, Robert, used to have the third bedroom, but he gave it up to my Mother. So Mother again has a place to put things we brought in our big steamer trunk and my ammunition box that's almost as big.

Robert and I sleep in the living room. We trade beds. One night, he sleeps on the couch and I sleep on his army cot. The next night we change.

Robert has an army cot because he was with the American army fighting the Nazis in Europe. He doesn't like to talk about the war. Too many of his army friends died there.

Robert's sister Ruth lives in a separate apartment downstairs. She and her husband, Herb, are expecting a baby soon.

As it turned out, I did get a job selling newspapers. I have a paper route for the *Cleveland Press,* which comes out in the afternoons. People don't look down on newspaper boys, as I had feared. My customers and I like each other, but the work is interfering with my after-school activities. So I'm going to change to the *Cleveland Plain Dealer,* which comes out in the mornings. I can deliver that early, before school.

I am going to Patrick Henry Junior High School. It wasn't easy for me there at first. My English had been good enough for talking to the Scottish soldiers during the war, but it wasn't nearly good enough for understanding the teachers in class. No one helped me with my lessons—no one even talked to me outside of class.

Posing in my bar mitzvah suit.

People talk a different kind of English here, which was confusing. Half of the kids in school are black skinned, which I had never experienced. All the boys do sports, none of which I had ever learned.

I was frustrated. Everything seemed strange. My family had to push me out the door every morning when it was time to leave for school. I cried at the thought of spending another day in that place.

Now it's already better. I have a new homeroom teacher, who takes me aside and explains the lessons I couldn't understand in class. One Sunday, she and her boyfriend even took me to a golf driving range, which I had never been to before. I am even preparing for my bar mitzvah.

I am also making new friends my age. The family of one new friend took me downtown in Cleveland to see *Guys and Dolls*. I had never seen a musical before, and I was fascinated. Life in America is different than it was in Holland. There still are many things I have to get used to, I know, but I feel that I'll be okay here in the end.

Postscript

Irene Heppner, upon coming to the United States at age 42, started a career as a librarian in various art museums. She never remarried but lived an active professional and social life. She remained in constant touch with the Janssens and visited them repeatedly both in Brazil and in Holland. She died in 1997 at age 93 in Mitchellville, MD, near Washington, DC.

A reunion in Kansas in 1972 with Heinz and Lou (foreground) and Annie Janssen and Irene (rear)

Heinz and Elli Graumann returned to Amsterdam, where Elli soon died tragically, ever haunted by her memories of the Holocaust. Heinz remarried, and he and his new wife, Lou, moved to the United States, where he resumed his work in psychiatry with the police department in Topeka, KS. Even though we kept contact over the years, Heinz never talked about Michael with Peter and Marianne, the two children he had with Lou. Heinz died in 1990 in Topeka, KS, at age 90.

Jacob (Opa) Kramer, my grandfather, was hauled from his old age home to the Sobibor concentration camp in Poland. He survived the hardship in a cattle car and was murdered at the camp by the Nazis on March 13, 1943, at age 74.

Harry Janssen took his whole family to Brazil in 1950 after his farm buildings, including the chicken-house, were destroyed by fire. They lived in a remote village along with a group of other farmers from Holland. Harry went back to Holland to retire and lived in a townhouse near his old farm in the *Voorpeel.* He kept a hive or two of bees there until his death in 1975.

Harry Janssen back in Holland in 1971

Dina Janssen continued living in Holland after her husband died. She finally found some peace there after having worked incredibly hard as a farm wife and mother her whole life. She enjoyed the presence of her children, most of whom came back to Holland with her, as well as her grandchildren. She died in 1998 at age 92.

Dina Janssen with her pet dog in 1996.

The Janssen children (there once were 10, but now only two survive) themselves had many children and grandchildren; most live in Holland. They all know the story of how their family rescued Jews during the Holocaust. The family was honored with a medal from the State of Israel and with plaques both at the Yad VaShem Holocaust Museum in Israel and in the U.S. Holocaust Memorial Museum in Washington.

A reunion with two surviving Janssen children in 2018. L-R: Ria Janssen van Ooijen (born to Dina in 1947); Reni Janssen, wife of Martin; Martin Janssen; and the author.

Frans and Ans Burbach in 1981.

Ans and Frans Burbach kept in constant touch with the Heppners the rest of their lives. We visited back and forth, and our correspondence in between visits fills a whole file drawer. Ans spent her time doing volunteer work. Frans rose to the position of Vice-President of what is now the ING Bank. They enjoyed a long retirement in the countryside near Amsterdam, where the Heppners visited them frequently until 1996, the year Frans died.

Jose Peerebooms and Henk Brandhorst, the two men who murdered Michael Graumann, were both put on trial for their double-dealing activities during the Holocaust. Jose was convicted and executed after a secret trial held by the Dutch resistance in 1943, while the Nazis were still in power. Henk had a civil trial after Liberation, and he spent three years in prison. He died in his native Kockengen in 1993.

Spot on a farm near Deurne, where Jose was executed.

Peter Kooter, who rebuilt the Janssen farm, with the author in 2018

About the Author

Max Amichai Heppner

A Massachusetts student made a tee-shirt for the author to identify him as a survivor.

The Holocaust engulfed the first 11 years of my life, and I felt the impact as a huge, ill defined, fearful fog. At the time, during the years 1933 to 1944, the adults around me did little to clear up the fog, so I retreated into my own world. I drew pictures and made up stories.

My mother and I moved to the United States in 1946, two years after we were liberated from Nazi oppression. During the next decades, I tried to figure out internally what had really happened during the Holocaust while the outer details of my life started taking shape.

I completed junior high and high school in Cleveland, Ohio. I then went on to get a Bachelor's degree in economics from the Ohio State University and a Master's degree in journalism from the University of Wisconsin. After that, my working life was spent mainly as a public affairs specialist for the U.S. Department of Agriculture, in and around Washington, DC.

In 1979, when my only daughter was born, we gave her a Hebrew name, *Liora,* which means "You are my light." That led me to also want a new Hebrew name. In the light of my personal history, I chose *Amichai,* which means "My people live."

Another book I wrote, *A Vision of Love,* is a sort-of sequel to this Chickenhouse story. This book takes an unflinching look at how I feel about being an American Jew in a basically Christian society. I followed that with *Unexpected Encounters,* fictionalized short stories revealing how often I've been put into challenging situations that I survived thanks to incredible luck, loving support, and sustaining insights. I've also recently published my father's story, *The Submergers.* It presents his take on the events that transpired in the Chickenhouse book plus some of his earlier history, including his flight from Germany.

As I'm completing the third edition of this book, I live retired on the beach in south Florida. I am married to Helena, nee Levine, and keep in touch frequently with my daughter, Liora, who now lives with her husband and two children in Switzerland.

After retiring to Florida, I have been teaching school children about my life in the chickenhouse, and they get it at a deep level. In the photo on the previous page, I wear a tee-shirt made by Tyler Snodgrass of Mrs. Sally Rubin's Fifth Grade Class in Burlington, Massachusetts, which studied with me for a year. At the end, they made a book of Holocaust poems. This is Tyler's:

NO!!!!

I am not yours to control.

I am my own person.

I will not give up.

I will not be taken away.

I will not let them win.

I am going to be strong.

I am going to have faith

I am going to be brave.

I am going to live my life.